THE UNITED ARAB EMIRATES

The United Arab Emirates

An Economic and Social Survey

Second Edition

K.G. FENELON

Longman
London and New York

LONGMAN GROUP LTD
LONDON AND NEW YORK

*Associated companies, branches and
representatives throughout the world*

First published 1973
Second impression (with minor revisions) 1974
Second edition 1976

ISBN 0 582 78066 7

Library of Congress Cataloging in Publication Data
Fenelon, Kevin Gerard, 1898–
   The United Arab Emirates.

   Bibliography: p. *111*
   Includes index.
   1. United Arab Emirates—Economic conditions.
2. United Arab Emirates—Social conditions.
HC497.T8F46   1976   330.9'53'5   75–42139
ISBN 0-582-78066-7

Printed in Great Britain by Butler & Tanner Ltd,
Frome and London

Contents

Note on Currency

DH = Dirham
BD = Bahrain Dinar
QDR = Qatar Dubai Riyal (Ten QDR = One BD)
The currency now circulating throughout the United Arab Emirates is the Dirham (DH), which is divided into 100 Fils. This currency was introduced on 19 May 1973, and superseded both the BD, which circulated in Abu Dhabi, and the QDR, which circulated in the other six Emirates.

Bahrain Dinars and Qatar Dubai Riyals were exchanged at any bank between May and October 1973 without commission of any kind, at the rate of ten Dirhams for one Bahrain Dinar and one Dirham for one Qatar Dubai Riyal. In November 1973 the BD and the QDR became foreign currencies subject to exchange fluctuations and commission.

The Dirham was given a parity value of 0·186621 grammes of fine gold and was equivalent to 0·21 SDR. Ten Dirhams were approximately equal to £1 Sterling, but the rate is subject to exchange fluctuations.

Chapter 1

Introduction

Great changes have taken place during the past few years in the Arabian Peninsula, and particularly in the emirates, or shaikhdoms—the terms are interchangeable—bordering the Arabian Gulf. The United Arab Emirates, or UAE for short, date back as a political entity only to 4 December 1971. Formerly known for historical reasons as the Trucial States, the UAE is a federation of seven emirates and covers an area of some 30,000 square miles, about the same as Austria, and has a population of about 656,000, approximately the same as Luxembourg.

All the seven emirates are coastal settlements except in so far as some of them have inland enclaves surrounded by the territories of one or more of the other emirates. Six lie on the southern shores of the Gulf and present a continuous coastline stretching some 400 miles from near the base of the Qatar Peninsula in the west to the Musandum Peninsula in the east.

These six emirates in geographical order from west to east are:

Abu Dhabi: The largest in area, rich in oil.
Dubai: Active in trade and commerce and the most densely populated. Dubai became an exporter of crude oil in 1969.
Sharjah: The third largest both in population and area. Sharjah possesses important settlements on the Batinah Coast at Khor Fakkan, Kalba, and Dibba. Sharjah in 1974 also became an exporter of crude oil.
Ajman: The smallest of the seven, with an area of about 100 square miles and a population of about 22,000. It is surrounded on the landward side by Sharjah but owns small fertile enclaves at Manama and Masfut.
Um al Quaiwain: Somewhat larger in area than Ajman though not in population, it depends like Ajman largely on its fisheries. It has an enclave at Falaj al Mu'alla, which is a small fertile oasis. It shares 30 per cent of Sharjah's oil revenues.

Ras al Khaimah: The most northerly of the emirates, it is the most fertile of them all, with a background of mountains and lush vegetation. It exports fruit, vegetables, fish, and some livestock. It supplied the rock to build Abu Dhabi's harbour and breakwater.

The seventh emirate, **Fujairah,** is the only one of the seven to be situated entirely on the Batinah Coast with no direct access of its own to the Arabian Gulf. Mountainous inland, it has a fertile coastal strip and excellent fishing.

POLITICAL DIVISIONS

Politically, the shaikhdoms of Trucial Oman presented an extraordinary patchwork quilt of intermingled states with numerous enclaves and dependencies intruding into one another's territory or even dividing a shaikhdom into two or more parts. In the past, clearly defined boundaries between the shaikhdoms were of little consequence except in settled agricultural land or fishing villages. Nomads, with their herds of camels or flocks of sheep and goats, roamed over the desert more or less at will, much as ships sail the high seas. Tribal limits for the use of pastures, grazings, or wells were vaguely recognized but less so than in other desert areas of the world. Even the shaikhdoms themselves varied in number and extent. There have been many reshufflings even in comparatively recent times. Ras al Khaimah, independent from 1866, was re-incorporated into Sharjah at the beginning of the present century, but became independent again in 1921. Kalba, on the Batinah Coast, claimed to be an independent shaikhdom and was so recognized by the British government in 1936, but was re-incorporated into Sharjah in 1952. Fujairah, youngest of the Trucial States, secured recognition of its independence only as recently as 1952.

Transition from tribal organization to statedom has never in the past been a matter of logic or of political map-drawing in Trucial Oman, and for this reason the area today presents its untidy but colourful diversity. The uncertainties occasionally lead to disputes such as that a few years ago over land in Dibba, an area on the Batinah Coast, which, small as it is, is divided into two parts: one zone, which is called Husn, belongs to Fujairah, and the other belongs to Sharjah.

THE ARABIAN GULF

The Arabian Gulf, or the Persian Gulf, depending from which side one views it, is almost an inland sea like the Mediterranean, though it is subject to considerable tidal variations. It covers an area of some 92,000 square miles and is 180 miles across at its greatest width, though only thirty-five miles across where the Straits of Hormuz give entrance to the Gulf of Oman and to the Indian Ocean.

Along the Arabian coast the seas are shallow for the most part, though in a few places there is sufficient depth of water to float the largest oil-tankers. The coastline is fringed with reefs, shoals, and islands. Navigation is difficult along much of the coast even for small native craft.

The Gulf is one of the most saline seas anywhere in the world, because of high rates of evaporation during the summer months, when water temperatures may reach 32° Centigrade (90° Fahrenheit) or more. The salinity is reckoned to be about forty parts of salt per 1,000 parts of water. The Gulf is not affected by the monsoon winds as it lies outside the area of their incidence.

The reefs, however, provide a suitable habitat for the pearl oyster, and for centuries the Gulf has been famed for its pearl banks. Prawn fishing, though very important to Bahrain, Kuwait, and parts of the Iranian littoral, is not possible along the coast of the United Arab Emirates, where the sea-bed is not suitable for the breeding of prawns.

Off shore there are numerous small islands, though in some places the sea is so shallow that it is difficult to decide what is mainland, what is sea, or what is an island. Many of the islands are little more than sand or mud banks rising but a foot or two out of the water. Most of even the larger islands are completely devoid of vegetation, though some have sufficient seasonal green growth to have made it worth while in the past to bring sheep or camels from the mainland for grazing. Some are inhabited during part of the year by fishermen, and in Abu Dhabi a recent count of these migratory inhabitants showed that they numbered some two hundred.

Some of the islands have attained importance. Outstanding is the triangular island on which Abu Dhabi Town is built and on which nearly two-thirds of the whole population of the emirate live and work. Another, Das Island, has assumed importance as the ocean terminal of the offshore oil company, ADMA. Another island, Halat al Mubarras, has been developed into a terminal for a Japanese oil company working an offshore concession. Dalma Island used to be a centre for the pearl-diving fleets of former days, but now its inhabitants are mainly engaged in fishing. Abu Musa, recently prominent when Iran set up a base there, provided a source of red oxide, which has been worked probably since prehistoric times. Revenues from its off-shore oil field, which came into production in 1974, are now shared by Iran, Sharjah and Um al Quaiwain. Sadiyat Island, a mile or two offshore from Abu Dhabi Town, is now the location of an interesting project for controlled environmental agriculture, while also near Abu Dhabi Town is the island Um an Nar, which is of great archaeological interest. The Greater and Lesser Tumbs near the Straits of Hormuz have become a bone of contention through their seizure by Iran, whose claim is vigorously disputed by Ras al Khaimah. They are of strategic importance as they can control entrance to the Gulf.

GEOGRAPHY OF THE AREA

Geographically the United Arab Emirates are an area of considerable variety. The coast is mainly flat and sandy except in the Musandum Peninsula, where there are steep cliffs, and mountains rise a few miles inland. Broadly described, the Federation can be divided into several clearly defined areas. First there is the coastal strip bordering the Arabian Gulf, where most of the population live. The coastal sands and the *subkhah* (salty sands) merge into a belt of desert and scrub which in turn gives place to a broad gravel plain, narrowing in the north of Ras al Khaimah, where the hills come down almost to the sea. Then there is the eastern mountain range, which runs for about fifty miles north and south and is about twenty miles across. The highest peaks rise to some 7,000 or 8,000 feet, though in the Sultanate of Oman they are still higher, reaching 10,000 feet. The western part of the Federation, including most of Abu Dhabi State, is relatively low-lying and consists of a coastal plain with an area of desert and salt flats inland. The topography is featureless and uninspiring, though on the road to Al Ain there are to be seen dunes of pink or red sand, often with beautiful patterns of waves formed by the wind. To the east, on the old road to Dubai, there are some remarkable examples of wind-shaped rocks, sculptured to fantastic shapes. Beyond the interminable sand dunes of Abu Dhabi and to the south lies the dreaded Rub al Khali (The Empty Quarter) described by Professor W. B. Fisher as "the largest and most forbidding of all hot deserts in the world". The desert served in the old days to isolate the coastal shaikhdoms from more powerful neighbours. The mountain range also served to cut off the Arabian Gulf states from the Batinah Coast. Access to the eastern side of the peninsula can be gained only through passes such as the Wadi Siji and the Wadi Ham; until the trans-peninsular road was completed, a vehicle with four-wheel-drive was required. The mountains and their foothills are scarred by numerous wadis, some very steep, down which, after rain, water may rush with tremendous force. In 1972 one such flood swept away a bridge in Ras al Khaimah Town.

THE OASES

On the coastal fringe there is a scarcity of fresh water, though inland there are numerous wells of brackish water with a very few providing sweet water. Though many of these wells are quite isolated there are a number of oases where water is more abundant and settled agriculture is possible. Among the larger oases, that at Al Ain in Abu Dhabi is the most fertile and extensive. It is roughly circular, about six miles in diameter, and contains ten villages, of which seven belong to Abu Dhabi and three to the Sultanate of Oman. The oasis is often referred to as Buraimi, but not very accurately as far as Abu Dhabi is concerned, as the village of Buraimi is one of the three in Oman; the other two Omani villages are Sa'ara and Hamasa. The villages located in Abu Dhabi territory are Al Ain (the main centre, and expanding now very rapidly), Hili (near which is an important archaeological site), Jimi, Qattarah, Mu'tarid, Masudi, and Mu'wiji. Jahili, with well tended gardens and dominated by a large fort, is sometimes classed as a separate village; so also is Muraijib.

The oasis is very fertile, being situated near a mountain range from which water is brought by a system of underground canals; water is also obtained from wells.

In Abu Dhabi State another important oasis is that of the Liwa, more than 125 miles from Al Ain. Topographically the two are quite different. The Liwa extends in an arc over a distance of some forty miles. Unlike the villages of Al Ain, those of the Liwa are not bunched together but spread out along the arc. In fact, the Liwa is not so much one oasis as a chain of some thirty small oases located in a depression, flanked by high sand dunes. Situated about 100 miles south-

south-east of Abu Dhabi Town, it is somewhat isolated by difficulties of communication. Limited supplies of water are available at a depth of from seven to twenty feet below the surface in small gravel depressions among the sand dunes. Date palms thrive on the lower slopes of the dunes and in the small valleys.

In other emirates of the Federation oases are also found, of which many are enclaves belonging to Sharjah, Um al Quaiwain, Dubai, or some other state intruding into or surrounded by the territory of a neighbour.

Sharjah possesses an oasis in its own territory about thirty miles east of the town, at Dhaid. This has an area of about fifteen square miles; on one side it is bordered by the Hajar mountain and on the other side merges into sand dunes. A few miles away in the same wadi there is another oasis, known as Falaj al Mu'alla, which belongs to Um al Quaiwain; date palms and fruit trees are successfully cultivated there.

CLIMATE

The United Arab Emirates lie within a sub-tropical, arid zone. In summer, especially on the coast, the climate is characterized by great heat combined with high humidity, as these areas are exposed to the influence of the Gulf and the Indian Ocean, though lying outside the monsoon area. There is a marked contrast between summer and winter months. From May to October, temperatures may range between 38° and 50° Centigrade (100° and 120° Fahrenheit) in the middle of the day, though they may drop to 20° Centigrade or even less during the night. In winter the range at midday is between 20° and 35°, with minimum temperatures dropping as low as 9° on occasion. (See Table 5 in Appendix B.)

Humidity is high throughout the year and this, with the high temperatures of summer, has given the Gulf a bad name for its climate; it is forgotten that the winter months on the whole may be quite pleasant. There are, however, considerable variations in temperature and humidity between the coastal fringe, the desert, and the mountains. Inland, the temperature, though high during the day, may be much lower at night. In the towns, air conditioning is becoming very general in offices, shops, and houses, even in small houses. This has made living in the towns far more tolerable, and indeed it would be true to say that living conditions as well as working conditions have been completely transformed by air conditioning. Now only those whose work keeps them in the open may be said to suffer unduly from the climate, though some too poor to afford an air conditioner have still to soldier on. Their number, however, is decreasing year by year.

Rain is infrequent and irregular; the rainfall practically never exceeds five inches in a year and may be as low as one inch or less. Rainfall can be very erratic and local, with places a mile or two apart having very different falls. As might be expected, rainfall is greater in the mountain regions. During the months of July, August, and September there is seldom any rain at all.

Dust storms may occur from time to time, usually accompanied by a strong north wind, but though unpleasant and sometimes severe they are far less intense than the dust storms of Kuwait. There, a motorist attempting to drive through a dust storm may find his windscreen pitted all over and the paint removed from his number plates. Daily average hours of sunshine vary between seven and twelve hours according to the season.

VEGETATION

On the coast of the Gulf and over the desert areas, natural vegetation is sparse owing to the scanty rainfall and the absence of underground water. If, during the year, rainfall is low, almost no vegetation is to be found. Indeed it might seem impossible for any vegetation to survive the harsh climate and the often salty soil. In the salt flats, of course, nothing grows, but in the sandy deserts, plants and flowers may appear almost overnight after the rain, capricious and uncertain as it may be. Desert plants are wonderfully adapted to their environment. Among the perennials some shed their leaves during the hot summer months, limiting loss of water through evaporation, while others remain green but protect themselves from loss of water by a dense covering of hair-like fibres. The cactus type of plant stores water in its cells and rations it out gradually to itself, even over lengthy periods of drought. Seeds of the annuals may germinate after a downpour, put down their roots, grow to maturity, flower, and cast their new seeds onto the ground to await the next rain, all in the course of a few weeks. Other plants have long tapering roots which reach down to underground water, while others of an entirely different type rely on a spread of roots near the surface over a wide area so as to utilize to a maximum any surface water there may be.

In marked contrast to the aridity of the deserts are the various oases, the Batinah Coast, and the favoured areas of Ras al Khaimah where water is available from the mountains. There, a great variety of fruits and vegetables are successfully cultivated.

POPULATION

Though much of the area of the United Arab Emirates is inhospitable, arid, and devoid of natural resources, there are considerable concentrations of population in the towns of Abu Dhabi, Dubai, and Sharjah. A census of the Trucial States was taken in 1968, the first of its kind to cover all the emirates. Since then the emirate of Abu Dhabi has taken a census of its own, in May 1971, and in December 1975 a second census was taken covering all the emirates.

The population of what now constitutes the Federation amounted in 1968 to 180,000, of whom 59,000 lived in Dubai and 46,000 in Abu Dhabi. Sharjah had 32,000 and Ras al Khaimah 24,000, but none of the other states had as many as 10,000. Preliminary figures for the 1975 census, issued in February 1976, indicated an increase larger than expected over previous estimates. The total population of the Federation amounted to 655,937. Abu Dhabi had the largest population, with 235,662; next came Dubai, with 206,861. None of the other emirates reached 100,000. Sharjah had 88,188, Ras al Khaimah 57,282, Fujairah 26,498, Ajman 21,566, and Um al Quaiwain 16,879. There were 2,372 citizens of UAE living abroad at the time of the census, and 629 could not be allocated to any particular emirate.

This growth in population has come partly from natural increase, and more importantly from immigration. Immigration has taken place on a large scale as a result of what economists have come to call the "push-pull" effect. Low wages and lack of employment in their own country have "pushed" many Iranians, Indians, and Pakistanis to seek employment in oil-rich Abu Dhabi or in the enterprising entrepôt of Dubai, where there is the "pull" of job-openings and relatively high wages. The situation is not unlike that of early 19th-century Britain, when the Irish came in large numbers. In our own day the same "push–pull" force has operated in Germany, where trade and industrial activity have attracted many workers from Italy, Spain, and Turkey. And just as the railways of England could not have been built without the help of the Irish navvies, so the infra-structure of Abu Dhabi or Dubai could not have been completed without the assistance of Irani, Baluchi, or Omani labourers.

A study of the censuses of the several states of the United Arab Emirates brings to light some very interesting demographic facts. In Abu Dhabi and Dubai, as in Kuwait, the most striking feature is the very marked difference in age and sex distribution between the native population and the immigrant population. The statistics of sex and age of the native population follow a typical distribution: a balance between the two sexes, and the numbers falling off in each successive age group. The expatriate populations follow an entirely different pattern. There are far more males than females and the populations are heavily weighted by the age groups from twenty years of age to forty years. Expatriates come and go and form a largely floating population. Individuals come to work for a spell of years and then return to their home country or move on elsewhere. They are normally in the twenty to forty age group; many are unmarried and many others leave their families in their home country, remitting to them a large portion of their incomes.

Another characteristic of the population of the emirates is that it is a comparatively young population, that is, there is a higher than usual proportion of young people. In Abu Dhabi about 38 per cent of the native-born population in 1968 were under fifteen years of age, and in 1971 the figure had increased to 41 per cent. In an older population, such as those of many European countries, the comparable percentage would be about 25 per cent under fifteen years of age.

According to the 1968 census, about half the total population of Abu Dhabi was expatriate: that is, nationals other than Abu Dhabian, or those of other Trucial States; and of these expatriates, 70 per cent of the males were aged between twenty and forty. In Dubai the pattern was much the same, with half the population expatriate and 54 per cent of the expatriate males aged between twenty and forty. The proportion of expatriates is now higher as a result of increased immigration. In contrast to Abu Dhabi and Dubai with their great demand for expatriate labour, the other states of the Federation showed a much more normal structure of population, with a rough balance between the sexes and a fairly regular tapering off in numbers in each successive age group. In Sharjah expatriates accounted for 27 per cent of the population and in Ras al Khaimah for only 7 per cent. In Fujairah only

2 per cent were expatriate. Among the expatriate national groups, there tends to be a certain division of labour. Broadly speaking—there are exceptions—the Iranis and Omanis tend to be manual labourers, the Pakistanis skilled craftsmen such as carpenters, the Indians clerks and shop assistants, the Palestinians government officials and primary school teachers, and the Egyptians secondary school teachers and more senior government officials.

Whereas in Britain females exceed the males in number, in all the emirates the number of males exceeds that of females by a small margin. This is also the case in other states of the Gulf such as Kuwait and Bahrain.

THE WORK FORCE

Construction gives more employment in the Federation than any other activity and accounts for about a quarter of the total work force. Government service comes next with about 16 per cent, followed by agriculture with 12 per cent. Next in order come the service industries, transport and communications, and wholesale and retail trading. The oil industry, though highly productive and indeed the mainspring of economic development, does not directly employ large numbers of workers and indeed it accounts for only 4 per cent of the economically active. This small relative and absolute volume of employment, however, is a measure of its productivity, providing the surplus and the foreign exchange on which the economy rests. Manufacture is represented mainly by small domestic crafts and by repair shops, and employs scarcely 3,000 persons.

The proportion of the population which is economically active (i.e. those engaged in working for a wage or salary or self-employed, but excluding those engaged in household duties and the like which, however important, are not classed as economic activity) has reached 43 per cent, a figure especially high when it is remembered that only 2 per cent of the female population is engaged in paid employment. The explanation of this apparent paradox is that among the expatriate population males predominate and over two-thirds of them are workers.

In the pattern of employment in the various emirates, there are major differences. In Ras al Khaimah, 40 per cent are engaged in agriculture, but in Dubai the percentage is only 2·3 per cent. Fishing employs 27 per cent of the total workers in Ajman and 16 per cent in Um al Quaiwain. In Fujairah, 64 per cent work in agriculture and 14 per cent in fishing.

Trade, transport, and services excluding government services account for just over half the working population of Dubai, while in Abu Dhabi the number engaged in construction is over 40 per cent of the total working force.

Chapter 2

Historical Background

To understand the present, it is necessary to know something of the past and of the historical influences which have gone to shape the present. It therefore seems desirable to include a brief historical survey of the area, though for our purposes it does not seem necessary to go back beyond the 16th century, when the Gulf came directly into the orbit of European influence. Portuguese traders were the first of the Europeans to establish settlements and to build forts for their protection. To these Portuguese traders, as to their later rivals and successors, the Gulf had become of great importance as it provided a link between the sea route to India or the Far East and the overland route to Europe from Basra. For more than a century the Portuguese were not seriously challenged by other European traders, and the importance they attached to their virtual monopoly is testified to by the elaborate forts they constructed, of which the best existent example is the Portuguese Fort in Bahrain, built on the site of an ancient settlement several thousand years old.

In the 18th century traders from France, Holland, and Britain began to infiltrate the Gulf and to attack the Portuguese monopoly in the furtherance of their trade with India. Eventually, the Portuguese lost their hold, and a long period of rivalry between Dutch and British traders followed. France entered the competition after the formation of her East India Company in 1664, but did not succeed in maintaining her foothold. Relations between the Dutch and the British appear to have been cordial during the earlier part of the 18th century, but early in the second half of that century they cooled and became hostile. The initial Dutch predominance was gradually whittled away by the British until in 1766 Dutch influence in the Gulf came to an end. Thereafter, Britain was practically unchallenged by other European powers. These latter were not, however, the only contenders for trade and influence in the Gulf; there were other powerful contenders, including Persians in the north-east, Ottomans in Mesopotamia, and Arabs in the west and south. The strongest local influence within the region was that of the Qawasimi, rulers of

Ras al Khaimah and Sharjah. Their influence grew as that of the Persians declined after the death of Nadir Shah in 1747. The Qawasimi built up large fleets and became successful traders and seafarers, though they also engaged in attacking British and other European vessels sailing in the Gulf. At the beginning of the 19th century their fleet comprised sixty-three large vessels and over 800 smaller ships, manned by 19,000 men. (See the note at the end of this chapter.)

In the interior there were also conflicts, and the Beni Yas tribe came to predominate and in the latter part of the 18th century reached the coast of what are now Abu Dhabi and Dubai.

British initiative in the trade struggle was not that of state or government but was the private enterprise of a body of merchants called the East India Company. This company attained an importance never before and never since equalled by a trading company, having its own armies and navies and conducting political negotiations with eastern potentates. Its name was a misnomer, as it traded with India and not with the East Indies. Eventually the political role, but not the trading activities, of the company were taken over by the British government.

During the 18th century, the lack of a maritime authority in the Gulf enabled the seafaring inhabitants of the coast to disturb traffic in the area by attacking not only the vessels of European traders but also those of Arab merchants. So prevalent did attacks become in the area that it came to be called The Pirate Coast. By the beginning of the 19th century the local fleets had become very powerful and well-organized. They were able to attack shipping passing through the Gulf without fear of reprisal and their success enabled them to extend their depredations along the south coast of Arabia and even to the Red Sea and the shores of India.

The southern coast of the Gulf was well suited to this, as the vessels used by the fleets could easily find shelter in one or other of the numerous creeks. As they were manned by large crews, they could use oars to propel their vessels when other ships were becalmed. Their technique was to overhaul their victim by closing in on both sides and grappling with the ship. Then the native crews swarmed aboard in overwhelming numbers.

Neither the **Portuguese nor the** Dutch had been able to subdue the raiders, but at the beginning of the 19th century their activities became so outrageous that decisive action to protect the Indian trade became essential. In 1809 a punitive expedition was sent by the government of Bombay in co-operation with the Sultan of Muscat, but after this expedition withdrew attacks were resumed and continued much as before. The Wahhabi invasion of Oman in 1800 to 1803 led to piracy on a still wider scale, and attacks on British shipping exasperated the East India Company to such an extent that they dispatched a large naval and military force in 1820 to destroy the pirate fleets and their bases. The town of Ras al Khaimah, then the most important pirate stronghold, was attacked, and its ships were burned and the fort demolished. Other pirate lairs on the coast were then destroyed or threatened with destruction. Fearing such reprisals, the Shaikh of Dubai and other rulers signed a treaty agreeing not to interfere with freedom of navigation.

This treaty was followed in 1835 by another treaty whereby the Shaikhs agreed to bind themselves to a Maritime Truce not to engage in hostilities by sea for a period of six months during the pearling season. The advantages were so marked that they were subsequently persuaded to renew this truce indefinitely. Finally, in May 1853, a "Treaty of Maritime Peace in Perpetuity" was concluded between all the Shaikhs of the Trucial Coast, as it was henceforth called. The peace was to be watched over and enforced by the British Indian government, to which the signatories were to refer any breach of the truce. Britain did not, however, interfere in any way with the authority or actions of the Shaikhs on land. Any dispute which they might have between themselves was regarded as their own affair, so long as they did not fight at sea.

Though Britain was ultimately responsible, the actual handling of affairs was delegated. Up to 1858, the East India Company conducted both diplomatic and administrative matters. Then the government of Bombay acted for the British Crown up to 1873, when the government of British India became responsible. After 1947, when India attained independence, and up to 1971, all negotiations and contacts were effected through the Foreign Office in London, which had a Political Resident in Bahrain and Political Agents latterly in Bahrain, Qatar, Dubai, and Abu Dhabi. By virtue of another treaty made in 1892, the British government had become responsible for the external affairs of the Trucial States, but at no time did Britain hold sovereign rights over any of the shaikhdoms. The conduct of internal affairs was in their own hands; it was only in external matters that Britain was responsible. The British government, however, had jurisdiction over certain classes of foreigners. This stemmed historically from the different legal concepts of European and local systems, but when modern penal codes were introduced, as in Kuwait, jurisdiction was passed to the governments of the shaikhdoms. The Political Agents acted as judges, and there was a higher court known as the Persian Gulf Court. All jurisdiction has now passed to the states themselves.

The East India Company organized its activities in the Gulf largely through the establishment of "factories" (offices and depots). These trading centres acted as distribution points for goods carried in British ships to and from countries in the area, and as centres for the company's dispatches going east and west. In these modern days of fast and easy communication, it is difficult to imagine how essential it was for a great trading enterprise in the 18th or early 19th century to arrange its own service for conveying its dispatches and commercial correspondence over a fast, safe route. Two such routes were available from India to Europe, one through the Red Sea and the other the overland desert route via Basra and Aleppo. The latter was the safer, and the countries involved, if suitably paid, gave protection to the couriers and to cargoes. This route became increasingly important in the second half of the 18th century.

SHIPS OF THE GULF

Pearling, fishing, and maritime enterprise created a big demand for ships and also for facilities for their repair. An important boat-building industry in response to this demand developed in Bahrain, Kuwait, Ras al Khaimah, and Rams. Bahrain seems to have been the cradle of boat-building in the Gulf, but though the ship-yards of Kuwait were later in developing they were flourishing before the end of the 18th century. Though all materials had to be imported, Kuwait possessed certain natural advantages for boat-building in its relatively dry climate and in the suitability of its shores for launching and repairing boats. The teak wood used in building the boats was obtained from the Malabar Coast and was found to season better in the dry climate of Kuwait than at other Gulf ports. But in all the shaikh-doms, teak was the favoured wood. Coconut wood was sometimes utilized but teak is the more durable, and, once seasoned, it does not crack, split, shrink, or alter in shape.

The boat-builders of the Gulf used no plans or blueprints but relied on their ex-perience and on the traditional skills of the shipwrights. In earlier times the boats were made from planks "sewn" together with fibre rope. The sides were carvel-built, that is, the planks were laid edge to edge and did not overlap. Holes were bored at intervals near the edges of adjacent planks and stitched by passing a large needle through these holes. Later, iron nails were employed to fasten the planks, but iron was scarce in the Gulf and was expensive to import. Eventually the Kuwaitis and other boat-builders began to manufacture their own nails. Some, six inches or so in length with large heads, were made in the shipyards and in the *suqs* (bazaars) by hammering heated metal blanks in a mould. Such nails were also used in house-building, as for example in making the nail-studded doors which are so attractive a feature of older houses in the Gulf. Many types of boat were con-structed in the Gulf shipyards, each known by its own special name which was de-scriptive of the shape of the hull rather than of the rig. The *Baghala* was the largest sea-going vessel, but eventually this went out of use and the *Boom* took its place. *Booms* were used for carrying cargo and were a very sea-worthy type of vessel with generally two, but occasionally three, masts. They had pointed sterns and were faster than the *Baghala*, which had a square stern. The sterns were often decorated with elaborate carving or were brightly painted. Another type of boat, known as the *Sambuq*, was used for pearling. This would be equipped with a special type of oar called *suff*, which was used to propel the boat slowly over the pearling banks. In Fujairah and Sharjah small boats of traditional design are still being built, including some of a very primitive type constructed from the stems of the palm tree. Used by fishermen, these boats are known as *Shasha*. Illustrative of the scarcity of iron in the Gulf are the stone anchors, made all in one piece with a hole in the shaft for the rope and having two broad prongs much of the usual anchor shape. Examples are to be seen in Bahrain, and it is probable that they were also used in the other Gulf states.

NAVIGATION IN THE GULF

Ships sailing along the Arabian coast of the Gulf were faced with many hazards because of the numerous shoals, reefs, sandbanks, and half-sunken islands. The uncharted coastline was especially dangerous and difficult to navigate for ships other than those manned by crews born and bred in the area. In attack or pursuit, knowledge of the intricate coastline was essential to the safety of a ship, as it could so easily run aground, whereas the native vessels probably drew less water and their pilots knew every yard of the coast. In 1820, after the conclusion of the third expedition against the pirates, a detailed survey of the Gulf was undertaken by Indian naval ships, under the command of Captain P. Maughan, assisted by Lieutenant J. M. Gray. The latter was succeeded by Lieutenant G. B. Brucks, who completed the survey in 1825 in the face of great difficulties and hardships. Further surveys followed, and in 1860 a general chart of the Gulf in two sheets was published as a result of the labours of Captain C. Constable assisted by Lieutenant A. W. Stiffe. Made readily available to all who required them, these charts were a magnificent contribution to the safety of navigation in the Gulf.

Ships needed further assistance, even after the charts had become available and after the risk from attack had been eliminated, if they were to avoid the perils of navigation in the area. Dangerous spots needed to be lighted and channels needed to be marked out by buoys. This task was undertaken by private enterprise in default of government action, the initiative coming from the British India Steam Navigation Company. Lighthouses were set up on islands, headlands, and anchorages, while shoals and channels were buoyed. Regular patrols by a tender ensured the maintenance of the lights and buoys. In 1910, the government of India took over the service and established a fund to meet the expenses, which was financed by dues collected from ocean-going vessels passing through the Gulf. After India became independent, a non-profit-making company called the Persian Gulf Lighting Service was incorporated in London in January 1950 to administer the service. This body was empowered to collect light-dues as before from ocean-going vessels visiting Gulf ports. Local craft received the benefits free of charge.

The Persian Gulf Lighting Service was governed by a Board of Directors sitting in London and representing the Ministry of Transport and the principal shipping companies operating to and from the Gulf. Its operational base was set up on Bahrain Island in 1952 because of the central position of that island in the Gulf. A lighthouse tender, the ss *Relume* of 1,500 tons, was purchased to service, replenish, and maintain the numerous but widely scattered navigation aids for which it was responsible. Two years later, the Service assumed entire responsibility for all lights in the Gulf, including those which had previously remained with the Basra Port Directorate.

After the Second World War, the great expansion of the oil industry in the Gulf brought about a considerable increase in the number and size of oil-tankers. To meet the consequent demand for more and better navigational aids, the Service adopted a policy of continuous expansion, and the thirty aids which it had inherited were increased to nearly 200, including two manned lighthouses, several major shore lights, a radio beacon, and numerous light beacons and lighted buoys. The majority of the lights are operated by acetylene gas which is manufactured in Bahrain by the Service itself. Gas lighting is favoured because of its simplicity and reliability, though a few of the navigational aids are operated by electric batteries and one on a remote and relatively inaccessible islet is worked by solar power.

In June 1966 the name of the Service was changed to the Middle East Navigation Aid Service (MENAS) and this organization now has full responsibility for
all navigational aids in the Gulf except for a few local aids maintained by Port
Authorities, by oil company loading terminals, or by national authorities. MENAS
obtains its revenues from light-dues which are payable by ocean-going ships in
respect of each of their first six voyages in the Gulf in any one year; warships, sea-
going tugs, sailing vessels, and local craft are exempt from the light-dues, as are
ships putting in owing to stress of weather or entering the Gulf solely for bunkers
or stores for their own use. In addition to its responsibilities for the installation
operation, and care of lights, MENAS also publishes the only existing Gulf-wide
system of Notices to Mariners and Radio Navigation Warnings to Shipping. It
undertook this work because many of the fourteen states or territories bordering
the Gulf had neither the resources nor the financial means to set up and maintain
such services.

INTERNAL SECURITY

Though peace at sea had been secured by the Treaties, the same could not be said
about travel on land, which was much less safe. Not so many years ago, travellers
were liable to be robbed by bandits, and the risks and hardships attending desert
travel were still very similar to those described by Charles Doughty in his work
entitled *Travels in Arabia Deserta*, published in 1888.

Since the nineteen-fifties, however, peace has reigned in Trucial Oman apart
from occasional minor disputes. In order to help to maintain law and order a
peace-keeping force known as the Trucial Oman Levies was formed in 1951.
Later renamed the Trucial Oman Scouts, the force was recruited locally but was
largely officered and trained by British personnel who volunteered for the service.
Its formation was the first practical step to be taken by the Rulers to co-operate
with one another. The Scouts had their headquarters in Sharjah but operated
throughout all the shaikhdoms except in the towns, where the specific consent of
the Ruler was required.

The force started with one British and two Jordanian officers, with thirty-two
other ranks seconded from the Arab Legion, but within two years it had increased
in numbers to about 250 officers and men. By 1955 it had grown to about 500
and eventually reached a total of just over a thousand. In 1956, when it was re-
named, it was given the specific role of defending the Trucial States against aggression. In the meantime, the towns were organizing police forces of their own;
Dubai set up its own local police in 1956, Abu Dhabi in 1957, and in the 'sixties
police forces were established in Sharjah, Ras al Khaimah, Ajman, and Um al
Quaiwain Towns. In 1965, Abu Dhabi inaugurated a Defence Force of its own,
with army, naval, and air wings. Defence forces were also formed by Dubai and
other emirates, but in May 1975 it was agreed that all the military forces of the
Federation should be merged.

From its earliest days the Trucial Oman Levies were able to impose law and
order throughout the whole of Trucial Oman, so that it became perfectly safe for

the traveller to venture into almost any part of the area without fear of robbery or molestation of any kind. The only exception in those days was the Shihuh country in the mountains of Ras al Khaimah, where this tribe maintained a fierce independence. If you wanted to enter Shihuh territory the technique was to fire your gun in the air. If the shot was answered you went forward, if not you stayed where you were. There was nothing sinister in all this; it was like knocking at the door of a house which you would not enter until answered. As everyone among the Shihuhs carried a gun, it was nothing unusual to use it to announce arrival.

The Levies, later the Scouts, were not merely a military or policing force, they also acted as guide, philosopher, and friend to all. Once when the author was travelling with his wife from Sharjah to Ras al Khaimah before the highway was built, his vehicle became stuck in the sand but was cheerfully pulled out by a passing patrol of the Scouts in their Land-Rover, despite the fact that it made them late for their lunch. Today, only eight years later, 1,000 lorries or more make the journey each month from Ras al Khaimah or Dubai to Abu Dhabi, laden with valuable produce, without the slightest danger of robbery or of untoward incidents.

TRUCIAL OMAN AND THE CHANGING WORLD ECONOMY

Prosperity for the Trucial Oman coast in the early part of the present century depended almost entirely on the pearl-diving industry, but in the 'twenties this industry was shattered by the flooding of the market by Japanese cultured pearls, which could be sold much more cheaply than the natural product and which could not readily be distinguished except by the experts. World-wide trade depression in the 'thirties dealt another severe blow to the natural pearl market, as it destroyed the luxury markets in Paris and India for pearls. The Gulf states, not only those of Trucial Oman but also Kuwait, Bahrain, and Qatar, in consequence tended to lose contact with the outside world and to relapse into small fishing villages and desert pasturages. Alone among the states, Dubai was able to make some progress, which she achieved by becoming a commercial and entrepôt centre. Sharjah lost to Dubai her supremacy as a commercial centre, and allowed her port to silt up, but she obtained some compensation by being selected as a stop-over for the flying boats of Imperial Airways (precursor to BOAC) on their route from London to India, until the outbreak of the Second World War led to the suspension of civilian flying. Thereafter, with the development of faster and larger aircraft, her airport was no longer necessary as a staging point and became merely a small local airport.

The Second World War accentuated the isolation of the Trucial States, which were thrown back on their own meagre resources. No military or naval bases were established in any of the states apart from the use of Sharjah airport by the RAF under an agreement previously made by the Ruler. Some small revenues were obtained by the Rulers from 1937 by the granting of concessions to the oil companies, but all exploration was held up by the war.

After the Indian Independence Act of 1947, the Gulf could no longer be administered by Britain from India. Thereafter, all Gulf matters were handled direct by London. In 1946, the British Residency was moved from Bushire in Iran to Bahrain, in conformity with a change in British policy away from concentration on Iran to a greater interest in the Arabian peninsula. Political agencies were continued or newly set up in Bahrain, Qatar, Dubai, and Abu Dhabi. In 1971, when the British presence left the Gulf, the military bases in Bahrain and Sharjah were evacuated, the Political Residency became redundant and the Political Agents in Bahrain, Qatar, and Abu Dhabi became Ambassadors. The Agency in Dubai was transformed into a consulate-general.

NOTE

Arab historians have recently contested that what has been called piracy was rather a national reaction against European intrusion into the area. They claim that attacks on foreign ships were a form of retaliation, and that the operations were in the nature of a local war rather than piracy. Much of the research undertaken by Arab writers on this subject has not yet been published, apart from Abdullah Abu Ezzah's UAE: An Historical Survey, *pp. 19–26, published in Arabic by the Centre for Documentation and Research, Abu Dhabi, 1972.*

Chapter 3

The Foundation of the
United Arab Emirates

THE PERIOD OF TRANSITION

Great changes, political, economic, and social, have taken place in the Gulf over the past few years, and from about 1965 onwards much has changed out of all recognition. The British presence has gone from the Gulf after an association of well over 100 years. No longer are British forces stationed at Sharjah, which had been a British base since about 1958. Each of the seven Trucial States has attained full and complete sovereignty, not only over their internal affairs but in their external affairs and their relations with the rest of the world. Their jurisdiction over non-nationals as well as nationals is complete, whereas up to 1971 non-nationals were subject only to courts administered by the British Political Agencies, except in recent years for certain offences such as road traffic offences. The states' destinies are now entirely in their own hands, without shade from the British protective umbrella. Further, they are now banded together in the form of a loose federation and act in concert in many fields of activity both internally and externally.

Economically, there has been an unparalleled transition in local conditions since about 1965, though the pace of development has been very different in the various shaikhdoms. In particular, Abu Dhabi's urban areas have been transformed almost beyond recognition, first in the capital town and then a little later in Al Ain. In some of the more remote desert areas of Abu Dhabi, however, life is still not very different from what it must have been 500 years ago, but already in districts such as the Liwa the winds of change are blowing strongly.

Perhaps the most important factor of all those making for change has been the motor vehicle. Tracked or four-wheel-drive vehicles can operate anywhere except perhaps over the treacherous *subkhah*, but as more and more roads are built, ordinary cars and lorries are bringing the more distant parts within easy reach of one another. What used to be a five-day journey from Abu Dhabi Town to Al Ain or from Dubai to Ras al Khaimah can now be made in about two hours. When the author first visited Abu Dhabi in 1965 there was not a single yard of surfaced public road in the whole of Abu Dhabi; the only bit of made road was a short stretch within the compound of the Political Agency between the Agent's house and his office. The airport runway was a strip of levelled sand, the office a tiny shed, and the Customs and Immigration Offices a Land-Rover. Now there are many miles of first-class roads, much of dual carriageway or even four lanes, and there are magnificent international airports in Abu Dhabi and Dubai capable of handling the largest aircraft. Banks have proliferated. Flowers bloom the year round on roundabouts or in parks in the town, and green trees line a not inconsiderable length of the four-lane highway between Abu Dhabi and Al Ain. First-class hotels are to be found in Dubai, Abu Dhabi, Sharjah, and Ras al Khaimah. There is a casino complete with roulette tables and croupiers in Ras al Khaimah, and a Hilton Hotel at the desert edge in Al Ain; and there are night-clubs in Dubai and Abu Dhabi.

Social adaptation to changing conditions is naturally slower and more difficult than economic adaptation. Habits, social customs, and traditional ways of life are slow to change, but machinery, plant, and equipment can readily be imported if foreign exchange is available as it is in oil-rich countries, and foreign technical and managerial expertise can be hired.

Nevertheless, in the space of a few years, great changes have taken place and continue to take place in the social life of the communities in all the emirates. Ways of life are being rapidly adapted to the new age and this adaptation has undoubtedly been helped by age-long traditions of trading and seafaring, notably in Dubai. Past experience of this kind has made the customs and habits of the foreigner seem less strange and unfathomable than otherwise they would have been. Also, the presence of large numbers of expatriates, drawn from many nations, cannot but have had great influence in breaking down conservatism, old habits, and prejudices against other ways of life, such as might have been felt in more isolated communities.

The most important factor, though, has been the rapid spread of education. Schools have sprung up all over the area. There are now over 150 schools open, some of which are quite large. All the emirates have their schools, whereas in 1959 the schools could have been counted on the fingers of one hand. In an area largely bound in the past by tradition, the most striking feature of the educational advance has been the opening of schools for girls in all of the seven emirates.

Television and radio have done much to widen horizons, as these media penetrate into the home and thus reach all members of the family, including the women's quarters. The almost universal possession of transistor radios has brought the happenings of the outside world into relatively remote regions. In the towns, modern cinemas which show films in Arabic, English, and Indian languages are very popular, again providing links with the outside world. Merchants are well travelled, indeed they always have been, but now the number of merchants, importers, and agents with international contacts has greatly increased, and it is not unusual for them to travel abroad several times a year. Many now are bringing their families on visits to Beirut, Cairo, and Europe. In Oxford Street, London, ladies from the Gulf can be seen not infrequently in the summer doing their shopping, masked and veiled as they would be at home—a striking combination of the ultra-traditional with the most modern.

In brief, the ferment of change is spreading to all the emirates, to all districts of each, and to all classes. The surprising thing is the rapidity of the change and its ready acceptance. Modern mass-media and the speed and ease of modern air travel have undoubtedly made possible what only a few decades ago would have been impossible.

The amenities of life in the towns have been vastly improved by the increasing availability of electricity. In particular, air conditioning is helping in no small degree to tame the climate, which in high summer would otherwise be almost unbearably hot and humid. More and more offices, shops, and homes are being equipped with air conditioners, and they are by no means confined to the houses of the rich. Their use is spreading down to quite modest homes, and the importation of air conditioners and their spare parts into Abu Dhabi and Dubai is running in terms of value at over 20 million Dirhams a year.

Another valuable amenity, now largely taken for granted in the big towns, is the supply of piped water in ample quantities. Not so long ago water was a scarce and precious commodity and even that which was available was often brackish, but now the desalination plants using natural gas as fuel can cope with the vastly increased consumption of the cities.

THE PATH TOWARDS UNION

There was no overwhelming need and there were no urgent pressures for the Trucial States to join together in some form of federation so long as they could shelter under the British umbrella which protected them from aggression and handled their external affairs. When, however, it appeared that Britain might withdraw from the Gulf, the shaikhdoms had to have second thoughts, especially the smaller states which were so small as not to be politically or economically viable on their own. Traditionally, the very idea of statehood or of federation in the modern European sense was largely alien to their way of thinking. The desert was like an ocean highway across which the nomadic tribes could move at will. Their organization was tribal, and the ruler was not so much a territorial overlord as one who held the allegiance of several tribes or tribal groups. In times of emergency the tribes might rally round a shaikh of the strongest tribe, but the concept that the authority of a ruling shaikh "had a territorial extent as well as a personal one was brought in when the British gave the name of 'state' to the sum of political influence that one of the undersigning shaikhs could muster among the tribes. Previously, territory hardly came into the question of rule, but only the domination of certain strategic or economically important spots like anchorages, wadis, oases, water holes, and grazing grounds. In order to have free access to these points or to exploit them, it was necessary to be on friendly terms with those groups who had undisputed rights to them, or to make them pay allegiance, or even to make them accept one's domination. The vast stretches of empty desert or mountain in between remained in general undisputed, a thoroughfare open to almost everybody."[1]

With the advent of oil, the concept of the state with its territorial sovereignty assumed great importance and further strengthened the British idea of a "trucial state" which could negotiate treaties and preserve peace at sea.

A permanent British Political Officer was first appointed in 1948 and took up residence in Sharjah; previously the British Political Officer had been resident only during the cold months of the year. In 1953 the post was raised to the status of Political Agent and moved to Dubai. The Political Agent in Dubai was responsible for all the Trucial States until 1961 when Abu Dhabi was given a Political Agency of its own in view of the coming importance of its oilfields.

British Political Agents acted as representatives of the British government and were responsible for negotiations and contacts with the Rulers. Part of their responsibilities included the issue of visas and travel documents, and the conduct of consular affairs generally. The agents also had certain juridical functions connected with His (Her) Britannic Majesty's Court for the Trucial States. There were then two parallel systems of justice in the area. One was that of the Ruler's courts which followed the Moslem system of Sharia law in accordance with custom, though they also applied any legislation made by decree (*Ilan*) of the Ruler. After 1950 the number of these decrees greatly increased and served to modernize the states' legislation by bringing it into line with the requirements of the new age.

The courts administered by the Political Agents were concerned only with British and non-Moslem subjects. This British system was formalized under the Trucial States Orders in Council made in 1946, 1949, and 1950 under the Foreign Jurisdiction Acts of the British Parliament. Under these orders all persons other than Trucial States subjects were, in accordance with custom already long established, specifically made subject to the jurisdiction of the British Courts. A joint court was established to hear mixed cases in civil actions where the parties concerned were subject to the different codes. In Bahrain there was a superior court known as His (Her) Britannic Majesty's Court for the Persian Gulf, to which appeals could be made and which was presided over by a British judge.

In 1960 the Trucial States Transfer of Jurisdiction Regulation ceded jurisdiction of the nationals of most Arab and Moslem states (excluding those of British Commonwealth countries) to the Rulers' courts.

Gradually the British jurisdiction was eroded, as for example by the establishment of Traffic Courts in Abu Dhabi in 1966 and later in Dubai and Sharjah. Finally, the British jurisdiction was retroceded to the states when they attained full independence in 1971. The last case, an appeal from a previous hearing, was heard

[1] Dr Heard-Bey, "The Gulf States and Oman in Transition", article in *Asian Affairs*, Journal of the Royal Central Asian Society, Vol. 59, Part 1, February 1972, page 16.

in July 1972 in Dubai by the British Ambassador acting in his former capacity as Political Agent.

ANTECEDENTS TO THE FEDERATION

British relationship with the Gulf emirates was of a very special and indeed unusual nature. The states were never colonies and no foreign government like that of British India was ever established or even contemplated; Britain's interests lay in trade, in keeping the freedom of the seas, and in the suppression of piracy and slave running, though other powers were denied the right to interfere in the area. The Trucial States themselves were free to go their own way in their internal affairs. British interests, however, demanded that there should be some form of state organized on a territorial basis rather than by a fluctuating tribal organization, and hence encouragement was given to those Rulers who could speak with authority for their own area.

This having been established, the next logical step lay in federation, and this ultimate goal was anticipated long before 1971. The very names given to the area, The Trucial States or Trucial Oman, implied a recognition of their essential one-ness. The Political Residency in Bahrain covered the nine emirates as a whole and the system of jurisdiction just described imposed a certain degree of uniformity. Even more important in establishing a basis for common action was the formation of the Trucial Oman Scouts, a force which, as has been said, was never confined to any one emirate but operated in all the seven shaikhdoms. The initial objective of its formation was to protect the oil survey parties and to keep the peace throughout Trucial Oman—a task in which the Scouts were outstandingly successful. The force saw active service during the Buraimi dispute in 1956, but during the last ten years before federation it was never called upon to fire a shot in anger. It always used a minimum of force in keeping the peace and when acting as arbitrator in local frontier disputes.

The first important step towards bringing the Rulers together to consider common problems was the formation in 1952 of the Trucial States Council and its Development Office and Development Fund. Though the Council had no powers to enforce common action, as any action had to be undertaken by each Ruler separately, it did much to promote unity among the Rulers if only by bringing them together periodically to discuss their common interests.

Several bodies working in the area found that their activities of necessity cut across state boundaries, and this again was a factor making for unity. Among such bodies may be instanced the Kuwait Office responsible for educational and health services provided by the government of Kuwait to the northern states, and the locust control activities of the United Nations.

NEGOTIATIONS FOR FEDERATION

The idea of setting up a Federation of Arab Emirates in the Gulf developed out of the need to ensure the future stability, security, and prosperity of an area that shares a common language, culture, and tradition. Even more important was the fear that disunity might encourage larger and more powerful nations to claim rights, privileges, or even suzerainty over some of the shaikhdoms.

The matter of federation became urgent when Britain announced that the British presence in the Arabian Gulf would be withdrawn at the end of 1971, but the negotiations which eventually led to the formation of the United Arab Emirates were long drawn out and suffered many vicissitudes.

The first step towards implementing the idea of a federation was taken at a meeting held in Dubai on 18 February 1968, during which an agreement was reached between the Rulers of Abu Dhabi and Dubai to form a union between the two emirates covering foreign affairs, security, defence, social services, and immigration. The two Rulers further agreed to invite the Rulers of the other Trucial States to participate in the federation and to invite the Rulers of Bahrain and Qatar to join their discussions on the future of the area.

These invitations were accepted and all the nine Rulers met in Dubai on 28 February 1968 and signed an agreement for setting up a federation under a supreme council of rulers. This council in June of the same year appointed a constitutional expert to draw up a draft constitution and nominated a temporary federal council as the executive branch of the supreme council. Various committees were established to report on such matters as unification of education, health, labour, communications, currency, labour laws, and the adoption of a national flag and a national anthem.

By October 1969, considerable progress seemed to have been made, and in that month the Supreme Council of Rulers held an important meeting to study an agenda prepared by the Deputy Rulers. No agreement, however, was reached and a communiqué issued by the council stated that the conference was adjourned to allow time for consultation. With that curt statement, the movement towards federation seemed to have reached a dead end.

The Deputy Rulers of the emirates next held a meeting on 13 June 1970, in the hope of reviving the movement towards federation, but in this they were not successful. Various differences of opinion and the growing inclination of Bahrain and Qatar to go their own way as independent states hindered any further progress. In attempts to iron out the difficulties, high-powered missions from Kuwait and Saudi Arabia, as well as a British envoy, Sir William Luce, visited the Gulf and attempted to act as conciliators. As the date fixed for the British withdrawal approached and as it became obvious that the British decision was final, a greater sense of urgency arose. Shaikh Zaid took the initiative and in a public statement said that Abu Dhabi was willing to form and take part in a federation of any number of states, not necessarily the full nine or even the seven. Envoys were sent to all the Rulers urging them to make a final decision about the federation. In July 1971 Abu Dhabi introduced extensive administrative reforms in its own government to enable it to emerge as a modern and fully viable state when the British left.

In the same month agreement was reached at a meeting of the Rulers in Dubai, and six of the states finally announced their intention to establish the United Arab

Emirates. The seventh state, Ras al Khaimah, did not oppose but deferred its decision.

Subsequently Ras al Khaimah made an application to join the six and was formally admitted on 10 February 1972.

The United Arab Emirates officially came into being on 2 December 1971, and later in the same month were admitted to membership of the Arab League. Early in the following year, the UAE were elected to membership of the United Nations, becoming the 132nd member of that body; this may be said to mark the Union's full acceptance into the comity of nations.

Shaikh Zaid bin Sultan al-Nahayan, Ruler of Abu Dhabi, became the first President of the Federation, and Shaikh Rashid bin Said Al-Maktum, Ruler of Dubai, its first Vice-President. A constitution was prepared for the new federation, which had some 150 clauses, among which were provisions for the setting up of a Federal Cabinet headed by a Prime Minister. There is a Federal National Consultative Assembly consisting of eight members each from Abu Dhabi and Dubai, six each from Sharjah and Ras al Khaimah, and four each from Ajman, Um al Quaiwain and Fujairah. This assembly acts as a legislative branch of the UAE government and is charged with the duty of assisting the cabinet in formulating laws to be submitted to the Supreme Council of Rulers for ratification.

The federal capital is located in Abu Dhabi. Federal responsibility extends initially to foreign affairs, education, health, and essential public works. It also covers justice and communications. Finance is to be provided to meet the expenditure of the federation by a 10 per cent contribution of the income of each member to the Federal Budget, but up to the present Abu Dhabi has met the budget requirements in full.

In December, the Supreme Council approved an eighteen-member Federal Cabinet list submitted by the Union's Prime Minister (Shaikh Maktum bin Rashid, Crown Prince of Dubai), which included six members from Abu Dhabi, four from Dubai, three from Sharjah, two each from Um al Quaiwain and Ajman, and one from Fujairah. Half the membership of the cabinet was drawn from persons not belonging to the ruling families.

After agreement was reached on the formation of the Federation, events moved quickly. On 31 July, in agreement with the British government, British jurisdiction was retroceded and all foreigners came under the jurisdiction of the Rulers' courts. In December Britain relinquished control of the Trucial Oman Scouts to the Defence Ministry of the Federation. This 1,700-strong force is now known as the Union Defence Force and has continued much as it was before. Under the Federation's constitution, however, the individual members are entitled to maintain their own defence forces. Abu Dhabi has a particularly effective Defence Force covering land, sea, and air operations. Each of the other emirates has a defence force of its own, but these are now to be amalgamated.

Early in 1972 the Trucial States Development Office and the Development Fund were wound up and their duties and responsibilities split up among the new Federal Ministries.

The work formerly carried on in connection with education, health, and other services by Kuwait, Bahrain, and Qatar was transferred to appropriate Ministries of the Federation, and the Kuwait Office in Dubai was closed, but not before emissaries were sent to the states concerned thanking them for their past services.

In December 1971 the British Political Agency was raised to the status of an Embassy, and the Political Agency in Dubai to a Consulate-General. Mr C. J. Treadwell, former Political Agent in Abu Dhabi, became the first British Ambassador to the UAE and the first ambassadorial member of the Federation's Diplomatic Corps. Diplomatic relations at Ambassador or Chargé d'Affaires level were soon established with the other Arab nations and with other states. By 1975 there were twenty-six Ambassadors accredited to the UAE.

In April 1972 the Federal Council approved the first budget for the Union, covering the year 1972. Budget revenue was fixed at DH 201 million. For 1973, budget revenue was increased to DH 510 million, and for 1974 it was DH 1,692 million.

During the first few years of the Federation's existence there were separate ministries for the various emirates as well as Federal ministries, but in 1974 this duality was superseded and all ministries became Federal. The former emirate ministries then became departments. This reflects the trend towards unification and integration which has gained momentum recently and which will no doubt continue in the coming years as the advantages of a common unity become clearer.

Chapter 4

Economic Aid and Development

After about 1950 Britain began to assist the shaikhdoms in their economic development. This new interest was foreshadowed just before the outbreak of the Second World War, when Britain initiated what might have become a continued policy of helping the states to build up a health service, had not hostilities intervened. In 1939, the British government established a dispensary in Dubai and appointed an Indian doctor to take charge of it. Further development had to wait until the end of the war, when in 1949 a British doctor was engaged to organize and develop a new hospital then being built by the British government in Dubai. The next step was taken in 1952, when a Water Resources Survey was undertaken and a number of wells were drilled to provide drinking water. Surveys were also commenced of the creeks at Dubai and Sharjah, which were silting up. Then in 1954–55 aid was extended on a larger scale and a sum of £25,300 was paid out by Britain to continue the water supply projects including the drilling of wells in Ras al Khaimah and the repair of a *falaj* (underground aqueduct) at Al Ain. The hospital in Dubai was extended and improved, and a school was built in Sharjah which was the first modern school in the Trucial States. A further £25,000 was allocated by Britain in 1955–56.

In the meantime an important innovation was the establishment of the Trucial States Council. This council was set up in 1952 on the initiative of the British government with the aim of bringing all the Rulers together, and at its earlier meetings it was presided over by the British Political Agent from Dubai. The council was merely consultative and advisory and had no formal or written constitution. Any decisions that might be reached had to be implemented, if at all, by the Rulers themselves individually for their own shaikhdoms or where appropriate by the Political Agent.

The Council usually met twice a year and discussed among other matters the issue of travel documents, the promulgation of nationality laws, and measures to combat locust invasions. Important political questions were also considered, such as the prohibition of slave markets or the re-incorporation of the then independent state of Kalba with Sharjah.

The council had no funds of its own available to promote economic development, but was requested to advise on the allocation of moneys available through Britain's Trucial States Development Fund. This fund had grown out of the early allocations of the period 1952 to 1955. The projects financed by these grants had proved so effective and desirable that in 1955 a Five-Year Development Plan was initiated covering the expenditure of a grant of £450,000. The plan applied to only six of the states, as it was felt that Abu Dhabi would have sufficient resources of her own from oil development.

Expenditure was allocated as set out in Table 30, though it was not always found possible to spend the allocation in the allocated year, but the surpluses could be carried forward to the succeeding year.

The plan proved to be so valuable in promoting worthwhile development that at the end of the period a Second Five-Year Plan was approved, for which the British government allotted a sum of £550,000.

In 1965 Britain considerably increased her aid to the five northern states: by then Dubai as well as Abu Dhabi had sufficient resources of their own to take care of their development. The new grant of aid from Britain comprised a capital sum of a million pounds sterling, spread over a period of three and a half years, together with an annual provision of £200,000.

In 1965 the Trucial States Council was reorganized and the chairmanship was transferred from the Political Agent to one of the Rulers nominated by themselves; the choice fell in the first instance on the Ruler of Ras al Khaimah, Shaikh Saqr bin Muhammad. At the same time a Development Office was set up under the Council and a Secretariat with well-qualified staff was provided. The Council decided that all aid given to the Trucial States should be channelled through a Development Fund. The initial contributions to this fund came from Britain (£1 million over three and a half years), Qatar (£250,000), Abu Dhabi (£200,000), and Bahrain (£40,000). On the accession of Shaikh Zaid, Abu Dhabi contributed a sum of £500,000, and subsequently £365,000 in April 1967, £1 million in September 1967, and BD 337,662 in August 1968. Thereafter Abu Dhabi continued to act as the largest benefactor.

From its inception in 1965 up to 1972, when its duties were transferred to the appropriate Ministries of the newly formed Federation, the Development Office distributed more than £13 million in aid. Over 70 per cent of this sum had been contributed by Abu Dhabi and most of the remainder by Britain.

AID PROVIDED BY KUWAIT, QATAR, AND BAHRAIN

Kuwait began to help the Trucial States as early as 1954, when grants were made for the construction of schools in the area. On attaining independence in 1961,

Kuwait sent survey missions to assess the development requirements of the Gulf states and set up a Gulf Permanent Assistance Committee (GUPAC) to recommend and administer economic aid, such assistance being in the form of grants rather than loans and without any political or economic strings being attached.

In 1962 a Kuwait State Office was opened in Dubai to co-ordinate the educational and health projects financed by Kuwait in the Trucial States other than Abu Dhabi, which by then had reached a point of full self-sufficiency in finance. By 1966–67, Kuwait had provided aid through this office totalling over £1·2 million. In the educational field Kuwait's aid took the form of financing expatriate teachers' salaries and providing scholarships, as well as help in the construction of schools.

Much was also done by Kuwait in helping to provide medical services, and in this sphere the chief contribution was the building and staffing of a large hospital located in Dubai, where patients are treated free of all charges. Staff from the hospital serviced numerous clinics throughout the six states, which were visited from time to time by specialists from the Kuwait Ministry of Health.

Financial assistance to education was also provided by Qatar and Bahrain by providing the services of expatriate teachers, not necessarily citizens of the benefactor's own country. Qatar, which had close relations with Dubai's Ruler through his marriage, financed a number of projects in Dubai, including the building of the first bridge across the creek and the provision of a fresh-water supply for Dubai Town.

Saudi Arabia contributed to educational expenditure, but her main contribution has been the financing of the main highway from Sharjah to Ras al Khaimah at a cost of over £1 million.

Non-governmental contributions have included assistance from the United Nations towards an anti-locust project and a water survey. A small hospital staffed by American and Canadian missionaries was opened in 1962 in Al Ain, which has made and continues to make a valuable contribution to the needs of that area. In Ras al Khaimah there is also an American mission hospital which has built up a high reputation for itself, and its services are welcomed even by the fiercely independent Shihuh and Habus tribes.

THE WORK OF THE TRUCIAL STATES DEVELOPMENT OFFICE AND FUND

In the seven years of its existence as a corporate entity, the Development Office has had an impressive record of achievement, not by any means confined to a narrow band of activities nor to any one state. It has been responsible for the establishment of water and electricity supplies; health projects including among many others the Maktum Hospital in Dubai; cottage hospitals in Dibba and Ras al Khaimah; health clinics in the remoter areas; maintenance and expansion of the Agricultural Trials Station at Digdagga; a hydrological survey over the six states; a fisheries survey in the Arabian Gulf and the Gulf of Oman; trade schools at Sharjah, Dubai, and Ras al Khaimah; and the construction of the road between Sharjah and Dubai.

The budgets have been divided between allocations for a capital programme and those for recurrent expenditure. In the last programme, in 1971, the estimated capital expenditure for the two years 1971 and 1972 amounted to over BD 2 million. The largest single item of expenditure was that on roads (BD 532,000), followed by health services (BD 472,000), water supply (BD 355,000), harbours (BD 160,000), fisheries (BD 110,000), and electricity supply (BD 82,000). A specially large item was that for beach protection at Ras al Khaimah, which amounted to BD 200,000.

For 1971 the estimated recurrent expenditure totalled about a million and a quarter dinars, of which BD 344,000 went on health services and BD 318,000 on education. Agriculture received BD 280,000. An almost similar sum, BD 270,000, went to meet operational losses mainly on public utilities such as electricity and water, which are provided below cost. In addition to benefiting from cheap water and electricity, the public also receives many other services free of cost, including health, agricultural, and veterinary services.

It is not possible to describe in any detail all aspects of the work of the Development Office, but there are some which obviously merit description because of their importance or special interest. The following paragraphs attempt to cover those which seem to fall into these categories.

Malaria Control

While malaria is unknown in the desert regions, it is endemic in some of the northern mountain states. The Development Office in 1969 therefore secured the services of a malarial expert from the World Health Organization to carry out a survey of the prevalence and extent of malaria in the area. The survey showed that the disease was widespread but variable in its occurrence, with very severe incidence in parts of Ras al Khaimah and the east coast. Following the completion of the survey, a malarial control unit was established in mid-1970. The unit first set about determining the areas where malaria was endemic and then mapping out the breeding places of malaria-carrying mosquitos. It also studied the types of mosquito prevalent in the area with a view to their classification and to the mapping of their distribution. Trials were carried out with different insecticides to determine which were most suitable for control work under local conditions. Controls are now being gradually extended with the aim of covering eventually all the mountain areas and their villages so that malaria can be completely exterminated. In 1974 an anti-malaria unit was established in Ras al Khaimah.

Road Building

The Development Office has laid special emphasis on the construction of roads, as the improvement of communications is of prime importance in the economic development of the Federation and in helping towards unification of the area. It is not sufficient to build roads in the hope that they will remain usable through the years; they must also be properly maintained, especially as after rains flood damage may be considerable. Road surfaces in Trucial Oman can deteriorate rapidly if they are not properly maintained. Urban roads have been built in all the capital towns and important links in the chain of inter-state communications such as the Sharjah-

Dubai road have been completed, while a start was made on the east coast road and on the trans-peninsular road through the Wadi Ham. Up to the end of 1970, the Development Fund had disbursed over BD 870,000 on pioneering road works, mainly on these two trunk roads, covering work such as constructing passes, building retaining walls, filling, levelling, and culverting. In the early part of 1971, however, much road work slowed down or was even temporarily abandoned owing to shortage of funds.

Mineral Survey

The lack of information about the mineral resources of the area prompted the Trucial States Council to commission the Overseas Division of the Institute of Geological Services to undertake a mineral survey. A preliminary survey was carried out in the winter of 1965–66 and this was followed by a somewhat more detailed survey of the mountain region during the following winter. The report recommended further exploration, though it stated that too much must not be hoped about large commercially workable deposits. Minerals such as chromite, nickel, copper, platinum, bauxite, magnesium, and asbestos certainly exist, but the quantities available still remain to be determined. The largest deposits of chrome so far located are situated at Masfut and Manama and are estimated to amount to 5,000 metric tons each. Apart from red oxide mined on Abu Musa Island, all the mineral resources at present being worked are building materials such as stone, limestone chips, building sand, and brick clays. Marble is found in Ras al Khaimah and it has been suggested that these deposits might form the basis of a new industry in the quarrying, cutting, and polishing of marble.

Soil Survey

A soil survey was carried out during the winter of 1966 by a team from the Geography Department of the University of Durham. Their report stated that there are considerable variations in soils in the area and that such variations occur at short distances. Drainage problems, it was considered, are not likely to occur except in a few areas over the short term, but careful consideration needs to be given to methods of irrigation and to the quantities of water applied, because of the presence of fine silts in all the soils. The recommendations included plant diversification, protection from desiccating winds, and overhead rather than channel irrigation.

Hydrological and Water Resources Surveys

The Development Office gave considerable priority to water supply work in connection with both urban and rural supplies. A three-year hydrological survey was initiated shortly after the formation of the Office and a consulting firm was commissioned to undertake the work. By 1968 a well-boring and testing programme covering ninety wells was completed. Since then many more wells have been bored, and piped water supplies have been provided for all the capital towns. Digdagga, Rams, Sha'am, and several other villages in Ras al Khaimah now have water brought to them in pipes. On the east coast the Development Office has been active in promoting water supply projects, and many of these are now completed, including those for Dibba and Khor Fakkan. Rural water supplies up and down the shaikhdoms have been greatly improved through the repair of the *falaj*, the drilling of wells and the installation of diesel-engined pumps.

Health Services

The Health Department of the Development Office had as its aim the provision of free health services for the local people throughout the five northern emirates. In Ras al Khaimah Town, the hospital was equipped with more than fifty beds and supplied with modern equipment including special departments for maternity cases and child welfare services. Free meals are provided for all in-patients as part of the service.

Another hospital, that at Dibba, also has fifty beds; a health clinic at Dhaid acts as a medical centre for the surrounding villages, and the clinic at Sharjah has a complement of four physicians. Clinics have been established at Um al Quaiwain, Kalba, Fujairah, Abu Musa, Digdagga, Sha'am, Idhen, Falaj al Mu'alla, and Jezirat Za'ab. Even in remote or scattered villages such as Masfut and Haweilat, small clinics have been set up, and other villages are visited periodically by mobile clinics.

Technical Education

Three technical schools were managed by the Technical Education Department of the Development Office. The oldest of these technical schools is that at Sharjah, which was opened in 1958. That in Dubai was founded in 1963 and that at Ras al Khaimah as recently as 1969.

In October 1971, there were 386 pupils attending these schools; the largest being that of Dubai, which enrolled 244 students. Sharjah had eighty pupils and Ras al Khaimah sixty-two. In the previous year, the total number of technical students had been 313. All three schools provide a four-year intermediate course of which the first year is a preparatory technical course for all students. In the following three years the students specialize either in general engineering or in carpentry. The engineering students in their fourth year concentrate on one of four fields: (1) machine work and fitting, (2) motor vehicle maintenance, (3) welding and sheet metal work, (4) electrical installation work.

A three-year commercial course is provided at Dubai school for those students who have completed eight years of previous education. In September 1971 the Dubai school introduced a secondary technical course leading to advanced City and Guilds external examinations or similar qualifications needed to obtain entry to colleges abroad.

Admission to the technical schools is available free of all cost to Arab nationals from the Gulf. Students who show special aptitudes for teaching are given further training abroad to enable them to take up teaching posts in the schools on their return. Several have already done so and the principal of one of the trade schools is an ex-student from Sharjah who qualified abroad after graduating from the trade schools.

AID FROM ABU DHABI

Abu Dhabi, in contrast to the five northern states of the Federation, is a dispenser of economic aid while the others remain at the receiving end. Dubai, while not as wealthy as Abu Dhabi, having only recently joined the ranks of crude-oil exporters and that in a much smaller way, is so to speak neutral, in that she can now provide for her own development from her own resources.

Abu Dhabi, as outlined in previous paragraphs, was a generous donor to the Trucial States Development Fund during its existence. After the formation of the Federation she has contributed considerable sums annually to the Federal budget and has also given generously to numerous Arab and other countries less fortunate than herself. These international aid contributions amounted in 1973 to over a billion Dirhams and in 1974 to some four billion Dirhams. The 1974 contribution included 500 million Dirhams to the Abu Dhabi Fund for Arab Economic Development. This Fund is intended to help finance viable economic projects in Arab countries by providing loans on favourable terms including low rates of interest; in its constitution and methods of working it is somewhat similar to a Fund previously set up by Kuwait. Operations of the Abu Dhabi Fund started in March 1973, when missions were sent to Tunisia, Somalia, and the Arab Republic of Yemen. Subsequently other missions went to Jordan, Syria, Egypt, Bahrain and Mauretania. During the first year of its operations (March 1973 to March 1974) the Fund granted loans to eight different countries covering eleven different projects. Five of these projects were concerned with developing the infrastructure in Jordan, Syria, Bahrain and Yemen. These five accounted for well over half the total allocations, and the remaining projects assisted were concerned with industrial development, tourism or agriculture.

Chapter 5

Oil and Natural Gas

In the decade following the first exports of oil from the Trucial States, Abu Dhabi was completely transformed, and it is difficult now in Abu Dhabi Town even to remember what it was like in 1962, when there were no paved roads, no corniche, not a single block of flats, no international airport (only an airstrip), no harbour for ocean-going vessels, no hotels, and no telephones. But not only has Abu Dhabi been transformed; her oil wealth has contributed to the development of other emirates either directly through economic aid or indirectly through trade and through the opportunities of employment offered to people from the other states.

The search for oil in the Trucial States began in October 1935, when the Iraq Petroleum Company (IPC) formed a subsidiary which was named Petroleum Concessions Ltd. This new company in turn formed another company in 1936 entitled Petroleum Development Trucial Coast (PDTC) with a capital of £100,000. Within a year of its inauguration, a representative of this company visited all the shaikhdoms offering to arrange payments for concessionary rights to explore for oil and to develop production should oil be found in commercial quantities. In 1938, the Shaikhs of Dubai, Sharjah, Ras al Khaimah, and Kalba signed agreements granting such concessions in return for annual rentals. Kalba, as has been explained, was then an independent shaikhdom but was incorporated with Sharjah in 1952. The Ruler of Abu Dhabi, Shaikh Shakbut, held out for some time, but on 11 January 1939 he also granted a concession to the company. The outbreak of the Second World War in September 1939 put a stop to operations for the duration of hostilities, and in the years immediately after the war the oil companies concentrated their activities on developing their oilfields in Kuwait and Qatar, which had been discovered before the war. Oil exports from Kuwait began in 1946 and from Qatar in 1949. On resuming their activities in the Trucial States, the oil companies met with no success until October 1960, when it was announced that oil had been struck in commercial quantities by PDTC some seventy miles west of Abu Dhabi Town. In 1962, the company decided to concentrate its activities in Abu Dhabi in view of the good prospects for its Bab Field and the apparent absence of large oil deposits in the other shaikhdoms. It therefore relinquished its oil concessions other than in Abu Dhabi, and to mark this concentration of its operations changed its name to Abu Dhabi Petroleum Company (ADPC).

In the meantime a new concept was being evolved regarding the ownership of the continental shelf, which was a matter of great concern both to the oil companies and to those countries which bordered the seas. Hitherto, the sea and the sea-bed beyond territorial waters (whether defined by a three-mile limit, a six-mile limit, or otherwise) had been regarded as owned equally by all nations or incapable of ownership. The whole of the Gulf is continental shelf with no water deeper than 100 fathoms, or 200 metres, so the question of ownership of the continental shelf was of great importance to the states bordering the Gulf.

The claim to ownership of the continental shelf was first advanced in 1945 by the United States, and it was not long before similar claims were made by other countries. At the suggestion of the British government, at that time responsible for external relations, the Rulers of the Trucial States issued proclamations claiming ownership of the areas extending outwards from their coasts in the shallow Gulf waters to a median line between the Persian and Arabian shores. Their claims were not disputed, and the effect was to put at the disposal of the Shaikhs large areas of new land albeit under the water, over which they were in a position to grant concessions to oil companies, thereby gaining much-needed revenues to supplement their meagre resources. The existing concessionaries, however, were not so pleased, as they held to the view that their old concessions included offshore rights. In Qatar neither the Ruler nor the oil company could agree on the interpretation of the company's rights off shore, so the Ruler, with the company's concurrence, took the matter to arbitration. The arbitrators upheld the contention of the Ruler that the new areas were not covered by the company's concession. The Shaikh of Abu Dhabi and the company, Petroleum Development Trucial Coast Ltd, also went to arbitration to decide their dispute on the same matter, and again the result of the arbitrators' deliberations was that the concession was limited to lands under the authority of the Ruler at the time it was granted. After this successful appeal, the Ruler of Abu Dhabi granted the offshore concession to the International Marine Oil Company, but this company, after making some half-hearted attempts at drilling, withdrew from the area, and the relinquished concession was granted in March 1953 to another company, Abu Dhabi Marine Areas Ltd (ADMA), of which two-thirds were owned by British Petroleum and one-third by Compagnie Française des Pétroles. This offshore concession originally covered an area extending over approximately 12,000 square miles.

The two companies, ADPC and ADMA, continued to operate as sole concessionaires in Abu Dhabi until they relinquished parts of their areas by agreement with the government. In 1965, ADPC relinquished 13,000 square kilometres of its area, and in 1967 this was granted to a new company, Phillips Petroleum. Up to the time of writing, however, this company has not been successful in finding oil in commercial quantities. In the same year, an area relinquished by ADMA was granted to a Japanese company, Abu Dhabi Oil (Japan) Company, which has been more fortunate and went into production in 1973. Another Japanese company, the Middle East Oil Company, which obtained a concession in 1968 from areas relinquished by ADPC, has not been so fortunate and returned its concession in 1974.

Further areas relinquished by ADMA were taken over by three other oil companies, namely Pan Ocean in 1970, Total-Abu al-Bukhaosh in 1973 and Sunningdale in 1974. Of these new oil companies, Total-Abu al-Bukhaosh became a producer in mid-1974, with four wells having a capacity of 30,000 barrels a day. The number of wells will be increased to nine providing double the initial productive capacity. The short period elapsing between the company's formation and its entry into production is explained by the fact that preliminary surveys were available from the original concession-owner.

As a result of the adjustment of the border between Abu Dhabi and Qatar, the Bunduq field has come to be worked on a joint basis by ADMA and the Qatar Oil Company (Japan).

In Dubai, an offshore concession is held by Dubai Petroleum Company, of which 55 per cent is owned by Continental Oil Company, and $22\frac{1}{2}$ per cent each by Deutsche-Erdöl Aktiengesellschaft (DEA) and Sun Oil Company. Dubai Marine Areas Ltd operates off shore and is jointly owned by five companies, namely Continental Oil Company (35 per cent), British Petroleum ($33\frac{1}{3}$ per cent), Compagnie Française des Pétroles ($16\frac{2}{3}$ per cent), DEA (10 per cent), and Sun Oil Company (5 per cent).

In June 1966 it was announced by Continental Oil that oil had been found at Fateh some ninety-five kilometres from land. Dubai now has become an exporter of crude oil. All the other emirates have arranged concessions with various oil companies but so far none of these has found oil in commercial quantities, except Sharjah, which began exporting oil from an offshore field near Abu Musa Island in 1974.

POSTED PRICES AND CONCESSION AGREEMENTS

Though posted prices have played an important role in the oil economy of the Gulf, they have become out-dated as a result of participation arrangements giving national ownership of oil, and they are now a matter of historical interest. It may be of help, however, before considering the agreements between the oil companies and the rulers of the emirates to explain the concept of posted prices and to describe the general nature of oil concession agreements as they operated before 1975.

Posted prices are those announced, that is, posted, at a crude oil export terminal for sales of crude oil. They are used as a basis for calculating the income tax due to host governments. The price when multiplied by the quantity exported gives a notional income for the company. After deducting costs and expenses, the profit so calculated is shared between the host country and the company in the agreed proportions. From 1948 to 1958 posted prices represented fairly accurately the market price for crude oil, but since 1958 posted prices have mainly served as a basis for income tax assessments of oil companies' profits, and they no longer reflect the actual prices obtained for the crude oil on the various markets of the world.

Posted prices vary from field to field owing to differences in the crude oils obtained from the particular field, including such factors as specific gravities, freight differentials or sulphur premiums. For example posted prices effective on 1 January 1974 in dollars per barrel for three fields in Abu Dhabi were US $12·636 for the Murban Field, 12·086 for Um Shaif Field, and 12·566 for the Zakum Field. In general the posted prices for Abu Dhabi crude oils were higher than those of other Gulf States because of their lower sulphur content and their specific gravity. In 1975, however, owing to competition in world markets the differentials tended to disappear.

Posted prices sky-rocketed in 1973 and 1974 as a result of action taken by OPEC to raise oil prices. Posted prices for the Murban Field which were US $1·886 per barrel in January 1971 rose to US $12·636 on 1 January 1974.

Oil concession agreements are very complicated and are not easily understood by the non-expert. They are nearly always a compromise hammered out after long and hard bargaining between the two parties. It is rare for either side to succeed in getting the exact wording it wants. The agreements are not immutable and they may have to be modified from time to time to take into account changing circumstances which are bound to occur over the long periods, maybe as long as seventy-five years, to which the agreements refer.

The first break in posted prices occurred in 1959 as a result of the action of the US government in making compulsory what had previously been voluntary. Independent American oil companies which had hoped to sell their new-found oil in the United States had, as a result of this action, to find alternative markets in a hurry and to sell at any prices they could obtain. Prices in Europe dropped heavily, and in February 1959 the posted price of Middle East crude oil was reduced by eighteen cents a barrel, and then in August 1960 by a further ten cents. The host countries strongly objected to what they regarded as an arbitrary action which reduced their incomes. So in September 1960, representatives of Iran, Iraq, Kuwait, Saudi Arabia, and Venezuela met in Baghdad and agreed to maintain a united front by forming the Organization of Petroleum Exporting Countries (OPEC). They were joined later by Qatar, Algeria, Libya, Indonesia, and Abu Dhabi. OPEC does not negotiate direct with the oil companies, as that is the responsibility of the host countries, but the organization has increased the bargaining strength of the governments and provides them with technical support.

Among the main objectives of OPEC was the stabilization of crude-oil prices, and in this it has been very successful in that no reduction in posted prices has taken place since its foundation. Another main issue between the oil companies and their host countries was the treatment of royalties. Early concession agreements provided for the payment of royalties, usually 12½ per cent, on the crude oil exported, which could be taken in cash or in kind. Since the crude oil provided in kind could be encashed at full posted prices, which were above world prices, the governments invariably took the royalties in cash. The agreements specified that the royalty formed part of the governments' share of profits, but OPEC argued that it should be treated as an expense and not as a credit against income tax liability. In 1964 this treatment of royalties became generally accepted, to the advantage of the host countries. Similarly, a marketing clause in the agreements was modified from the original discount of 2 per cent off posted prices to one of 0·5 per cent thus again increasing the advantage of the host countries.

The rigidity of the earlier agreements has also been broken down in another direction. Originally the concessions covered the whole of a country's territory, or at any rate large sections of it, but this was felt to be unsatisfactory by many of the host countries and they demanded the successive relinquishment of areas not yet exploited by the company concerned. This demand has now been met in most of the Middle East countries by the oil companies in regard to their original concessions, and in practically all new concessional agreements clauses are included providing for relinquishment in successive stages. The trend in these new agreements has been towards more rapid relinquishment. In Abu Dhabi since 1967, considerable areas have been relinquished by the producing companies, ADPC and ADMA, and these relinquished areas have been re-allotted to other companies through competitive bidding. In the new concessions there has been a significant improvement of terms in favour of the government. Minimum exploration expenditure has been increased, as have bonuses payable at various stages of development. Various fringe benefits have accrued to the government, as for example an obligation to build a refinery or petro-chemical plants after production reaches a certain minimum.

Another significant trend has been the inauguration of national oil companies, that for Abu Dhabi having been established in 1972.

In January 1968, co-operation between the Arab oil-producing companies went a step further through the formation of the Organization of Arab Petroleum Exporting Countries (OAPEC). The founder members were Kuwait, Libya, and Saudi Arabia, and in May 1970 the three original members were joined by Abu Dhabi, Dubai, Bahrain, Algeria, and Qatar. At its foundation the new organization stated that its main aim was to promote co-operation between its members "in various forms of economic activity in the oil industry and the realization of the closest ties between them". It also aims "to determine the ways and means of safeguarding the legitimate oil interests of the members, whether individually or collectively, to unify their efforts so as to ensure the flow of oil to its consumption markets at fair and reasonable terms and to create a favourable climate for the capital and expertise invested in the oil industry in the member countries". Dubai has now resigned from OAPEC as the organization did not support the construction of its tanker dry dock.

Tons and barrels

Some readers may not be familiar with the system used to measure quantities of crude oil. Crude oil may be measured either in tons or in barrels. The tons may be long tons (2,240 lb), metric tons, now usually written tonnes (2,200 lb), or short tons (2,000 lb). The barrel is one of 35 imperial gallons but the number of barrels to the ton varies with the specific gravity of the oil, but as an approximate average there are 7·45 barrels to a long ton.

Production of crude oil is often stated to be so many barrels a day (b/d) and confusion sometimes arises when some data are given in tons a year and others in barrels a day. Barrels a day can be converted very easily though only approximately into long tons a year by multiplying barrels a day by 50. This factor is based on world average specific gravities. Thus for example 100,000 barrels a day becomes approximately 5 million long tons a year.

THE MAJOR OIL COMPANIES

Abu Dhabi Petroleum Company (ADPC)

The Abu Dhabi Petroleum Company (ADPC) is owned by a group of companies: British Petroleum Exploration Company (Middle East) Ltd, Shell Petroleum Company Ltd, Compagnie Française des Pétroles, and the Near East Development Corporation (an equal partnership of Standard Oil Company, New Jersey, and Mobiloil Corporation), each holding 23¾ per cent of the share capital. The remaining 5 per cent is held by the Participations and Explorations Corporation, successors to the original Gulbenkian holding of "Mr Five per Cent", who negotiated early concessions. It is now jointly owned by BP, CFP, the Near East Development Corporation and ADNOC.

The original concession of PDTC of 1 January 1939 was for a period of seventy-five years and covered the land, islands, and coastal waters of Abu Dhabi. Exploratory drilling began in 1950, but the first four wells were unsuccessful, though sufficiently encouraging to justify development of what has come to be known as the Bab Field. Further wells were drilled to determine the extent of this field, and plans were put into operation for the construction of the requisite production, gathering, pipe-line, and other facilities. It was decided that twenty-four wells would be necessary, of which seventeen were connected to a combined degassing and pumping station at Habshan. The other seven were linked to a remote first-stage separator unit at Shames, ten miles distant. After treatment to remove hydrogen sulphide, the oil is pumped through a twenty-four-inch main pipe-line traversing a distance of seventy miles to Jebel Dhanna, where a loading-terminal was constructed. In 1964, another field at Bu Hasa was brought into production and connected to the main pipe-line. A third field, further away at Asab, is now being developed, as is a still newer discovery situated between Abu Dhabi Town and the oasis of Al Ain.

At the Jebel Dhanna Terminal there are a tank farm and tanker loading facilities, which have been improved and expanded since first brought into operation and are now capable of part-loading the latest giant tankers. So far the largest cargo loaded there was one of nearly 140,000 tons aboard the ss *Zuiko Maru* and the largest tanker handled at the terminal was the ss *Jalinga*, of 258,000 deadweight tons, which loaded over 115,000 tons for Japan.

The operations of the company are conducted from three main centres: the Town of Abu Dhabi, where the head office is located; Bu Hasa, where production operations are based; and Jebel Dhanna Terminal. The older base at Tarif has now been closed down and the work concentrated at Bu Hasa.

The headquarters of the company were originally located in Bahrain, but in November 1966 they were moved to Abu Dhabi Town and the Bahrain office was closed. A new office block of modern design was built in the town and has now been extended. A staff house and accommodation to house expatriate staff and their families were also provided. The arrival of these expatriate staff and their families was the first major influx of foreign families into the town. Staff and employee strength at the end of 1971 was 319 persons, of whom 106 were specialists or administrative staff. This may seem to be a small labour force in relation to the massive production of the company, but its activities are highly mechanized as befits a country where capital-intensive industry is desirable.

Exports during 1971 totalled 208 million barrels (26·9 million tons), which represented an increase of 33·7 per cent on exports in 1970. Japan is the most important customer for ADPC oil and took 44·5 per cent of the company's total production in 1971. In addition to exports, 89,000 barrels were supplied to the government of Abu Dhabi for the electricity generating stations. Natural gas was also supplied to fuel the government's new electricity power station and water desalination plant, being transmitted over a special gas pipe-line from the separator plant at Shames on the Bab Field.

The original 1939 agreement between Abu Dhabi and the Abu Dhabi Petroleum Company (or rather Petroleum Development Trucial Coast, as it was then) provided for a fixed royalty of three rupees per ton, which was equivalent to about eight cents a barrel. On 19 September 1965, a new agreement was signed providing for a fifty-fifty profit-sharing arrangement which raised the Ruler's receipts to an estimated seventy-five cents a barrel, or about £2 sterling a ton. The agreement also provided for the surrender of 13,000 square kilometres (about 5,000 square miles) of concession area, followed by a further 6,500 square kilometres in September 1967, 9,000 square kilometres more in September 1969, and 10,000 square kilometres in September 1971. As a result of these successive relinquishments, the total area remaining with the company amounts to slightly less than 40,000 square kilometres, or about half its original concession.

On 10 November 1966, a new agreement implementing the treatment of royalties as an expense was signed, as a supplement to the 1965 profit-sharing agreement. Then, in June 1970, another agreement was arrived at which provided for the amortizing of exploration and drilling expenditure. In the following month, the company agreed to pay the Ruler's share of profits monthly instead of quarterly as before. In February 1971, the share of profits going to the Ruler was raised to 55 per cent of total profits. Payments to the government in respect of the Ruler's share for 1971 amounted to £111·1 million, about four times the amount paid in 1966.

Abu Dhabi Marine Areas Ltd (ADMA)

Abu Dhabi Marine Areas Ltd obtained its concession for offshore rights in 1953 and was the first company to discover oil in commercial quantities in Trucial

Oman. The discovery occurred in September 1958 at Um Shaif, about eighty miles out at sea, after a well had been sunk to a depth of 8,775 feet. From the Um Shaif field, oil is now pumped over a distance of some twenty miles through a submarine pipe to Das Island, which serves as the company's operating base, as its oil storage tank farm, and as a terminal for loading ocean-going tankers.

Das Island lies about midway between Abu Dhabi and the Qatar Peninsula and is about sixty miles distant from the nearest shore. It is roughly a square mile in area and consists mostly of sand, rising a few feet above sea-level except for some outcrops of rock which reach about 100 feet in height at the northern end of the island. It was a desolate, uninhabited place, rarely visited even by fishermen before 1965, when construction of the base was begun. All constructional material had to be brought from Bahrain, some 170 miles away, and nearly 500 workmen were required to convert this barren island into a modern oil terminal complex. Now it is a busy centre of activity with a harbour 1,200 feet long and 400 feet wide, an airstrip 4,000 feet long at the south end of the island, and with offices and houses for the staff. More than 800 persons are employed by the company on Das Island, and clubs and recreational facilities are provided in addition to living-quarters.

The tanker ss *British Signal* was the first to load Um Shaif crude oil from Das Island, to commence Abu Dhabi's meteoric rise to fame as an exporter of crude oil. This was in July 1962, and by the end of that year nearly three-quarters of a million tons of crude were exported from the island. By 1965, the annual export had increased to well over 4 million tons, and by 1971 the tonnage loaded exceeded 16 million tons for the year.

Das Island is also linked by a sixty-mile thirty-inch pipe-line to a collecting platform in another offshore field, the Zakum field, where exploratory drilling began in 1963 and which became a producer in 1967. The first cargo of Zakum crude oil was shipped to West Germany on 2 November 1967, and the present output from this field is over 200,000 barrels daily from its thirty-nine wells. Each of these wells has a three-legged well-head production platform complex with gas separators, a helicopter deck and accommodation for the staff. ADMA's fields, like those of its opposite number on land, are highly automated. The wells in the Um Shaif and Zakum Fields are monitored and operated by remote control through a radio link from Das Island. The search for offshore oil continued, and still another field was discovered at Al-Bunduq, lying partly in the territorial waters of Qatar.

The company's terminal facilities at Das Island, which consist of two conventional crude-oil loading berths and a single-buoy mooring, are capable of handling tankers of up to 300,000 tons capacity. The water depth at the two berths ranges from fifty-five to sixty-seven feet, and at the single-buoy mooring it is ninety feet. The company envisages a further period of sustained growth, and to this end a number of major construction projects were started in 1971, including the expansion of production facilities in the offshore fields and on Das Island.

The original concession agreement effected in 1953 with Abu Dhabi Marine Areas Ltd remained unchanged until November 1966, when a supplementary agreement was signed. The new agreement gave the Ruler increased royalties through the adoption of the fifty-fifty arrangement, with royalties treated as an expense in accordance with the pattern set in other Middle East oil-producing countries. The oil companies had been anxious for some years to move over to this arrangement, but Shaikh Shakbut had been very reluctant to agree. As a result of this and later agreements, and with greater production, the tax and oil royalties received by the Ruler from ADMA rose greatly. (For ADMA's exports of crude oil, see Table 8.)

ADMA was originally owned by BP and CFP, but at the end of 1972 BP sold 45 per cent of its two-thirds stake to a group of Japanese companies, BP receiving $780 million for the deal. The Abu Dhabi government objected that the company had not received prior permission, but this delicate issue was eventually ironed out when BP agreed to finance the 15,000 b/d refinery at Um an Nar, which was being built by Kellogg International Corporation. ADMA also provided the government with a $50 million interest-free loan in the form of an advance tax payment.

The New Oil Companies of Abu Dhabi

The two established oil companies, in conformity with their revised agreements with the Ruler of Abu Dhabi, were obliged to relinquish substantial segments of their original concessions. After these relinquishments, new oil interests obtained a foothold in Abu Dhabi. By 1974, six oil companies in addition to the two giants (ADPC and ADMA) had obtained concessions in Abu Dhabi. The first of the newcomers was a consortium composed of Phillips Petroleum Company, the American Independent Oil Company (Aminoil) and the Italian AGIP group, which was allotted a concession area on land relinquished by ADPC in 1965. The agreement was drawn up in the sophisticated terms of contemporary concessions in the Middle East and was in sharp contrast with the earliest Abu Dhabi concessions. Competitive bidding for the new concession had been very keen and had been stimulated by the success of the companies already operating in the shaikhdom. The terms were fully in line with the conditions laid down by the Organization of Petroleum Exporting Countries (OPEC). The Ruler will receive 55 per cent of profits calculated on the posted price of crude oil (including oil sold at lower prices), and in addition the royalty will be allowed as an expense in accordance with the OPEC formula: at a rate of $12\frac{1}{2}$ per cent on posted prices. The consortium agreed to spend a minimum of $12 million on exploration and drilling during the five years from 1967 to 1971, and to pay an annual rental until oil is discovered in commercial quantities, which was defined as a production of 15,000 barrels daily. Other provisions included an initial bonus of $3 million. Thereafter a substantial bonus is to be paid on the discovery of oil in commercial quantities, with further though smaller bonuses when exports reach 100,000 barrels daily and again when they reach 200,000 barrels a day. The Ruler has the right to participate up to 15 per cent in the operations of the consortium if oil is discovered in commercial quantities, and the group has undertaken, if requested, to market the share of the oil accruing to the Ruler from his participation.

Another new company, the Abu Dhabi Oil Company (Japan), has been more fortunate than Phillips Petroleum Company in its hunt for oil, and is now exporting crude oil from a terminal situated on the island of Halat al Mubarras which lies fifty-five miles west of Abu Dhabi Town. The company struck oil in January 1970, with its first two wild-cat wells yielding 3,000 tons of oil a day. With further wells sunk it was expected that there would be a producing capacity from the field of 200,000 barrels daily, but these expectations have not been realized and output has been disappointing. Storage tanks and other essential buildings have been erected on the island and the tankers load from single-point moorings. The concession area of ADOC (Japan) was originally part of that held by ADMA and in 1967 was awarded to the Japanese company, which is owned in equal shares by three companies, namely the Maruzen Oil Co, Daikyo Oil Co, and Nippon Mining Co. ADOC undertook to spend a minimum of $13 million on prospecting, exploring, drilling, and development within eight years. A signature bonus of $1 million was paid, and further bonuses of $2 million each were due on the discovery of oil in commercial quantities and on attainment of regular export rates of 100,000 barrels daily and 200,000 barrels daily. In other respects the terms of the concession follow the lines laid down by OPEC, though in addition there is to be a royalty of $12\frac{1}{2}$ per cent of the proceeds of any sales of natural gas. Any surplus of natural gas is to be made available to the government free of charge.

Another Japanese undertaking, the Middle East Oil Company, began operating on land in 1968 in an area relinquished by ADPC. The parent company was the Mitsubishi Oil Development Company, which is a group formed from five associated Mitsubishi companies. The terms of the concession, which was to run for thirty-five years, were somewhat similar to those of the other Japanese company, though more onerous. The company was committed to building a refinery in Abu Dhabi within three years of producing an average 200,000 barrels daily. It was required also to undertake feasibility studies for joint petro-chemical or other projects when production reached 300,000 barrels daily. Oil, however, was not found in commercial quantities, and in mid-1974 the company ceased operation.

In brief, the history of the new concessions in Abu Dhabi has been one of increasingly favourable terms for the emirate. Non-amortizable bonuses have become successively greater, relinquishment terms more rapid, and the duration of the concessions shorter, while various types of fringe benefits have been added. Other companies to obtain concessions were Pan Ocean (1970), Toral-Abu Bukhaosh (1973) and Sunningdale (1974).

Abu Dhabi during recent years has been one of the fastest growing oil producers of the world. In 1972, total production in Abu Dhabi amounted to 50 million long tons, whereas five years before, in 1967, it was only slightly more than 19 million long tons. In 1973 production had soared to over 61 million tons, including a contribution of 188 thousand tons by the Abu Dhabi Oil Company (Japan). In 1974, production was over 66 million tons (see Table 7).

Abu Dhabi National Oil Company

Abu Dhabi's own oil company (ADNOC) was formed in 1971. It now represents government interests on the boards of the foreign oil companies and has taken over the marketing of the government's share of crude oil received under participation agreements. The first shipment of participating oil was exported to Japan on 7 April 1973. ADNOC is now engaged in building up its own tanker fleet through its subsidiary, the Abu Dhabi National Tanker Company (ADNATCO) which at present is wholly owned by its parent company but which can sell up to 49 per cent of the capital to UAE nationals. This company purchased its first tanker in 1975, which is in the VLCC category, of 269 thousand tons. The tanker has been re-named *Al Dhafra*, after the district in the centre of the emirate which is famed for its grazing areas. Purchase of a second tanker of 260 thousand tons was negotiated in the same year whilst the vessel was under construction in a Spanish shipyard.

Local distribution of refined oil products, petrol service and filling stations were taken over in July 1973 by a subsidiary of ADNOC. The filling stations were previously owned and operated by three distributors, BP, Shell, and Caltex (Gulf). A further responsibility of ADNOC is implementing plans for oil-based industries in Abu Dhabi. The first project of this kind to be operated by the National Oil Company is the new 15,000 b/d oil refinery at Um an Nar, the island just off shore from Abu Dhabi town but now connected by a causeway. A number of subsidiary companies have been formed under the wing of ADNOC, including the National Drilling Company and the Oil Installation Company which undertakes the construction of rigs and off-shore well-head equipment.

Participation and the New Look

In 1972 four of the Gulf States including Abu Dhabi (the other three being Saudi Arabia, Kuwait and Qatar) signed a "declaration of intent" which provided for the eventual control by the producing state of the assets and output of the oil companies. Separate agreements were to be negotiated with each of the foreign companies operating in Abu Dhabi. As a first step, Abu Dhabi through its national oil company acquired a 25 per cent holding (or participation as it is called) in the equity capital of ADMA and ADPC. This gave the National Oil Company the right to sell on its own account a quarter of the companies' output in the world market. Alternatively, the oil could be sold back to the oil company concerned, which would then make its own arrangements for marketing. This first participation agreement with ADMA and ADPC was signed on 20 December 1972, but was followed in September 1974 by a further agreement which increased the government's share to 60 per cent, retrospective to 1 January 1974.

Dubai Petroleum Company

In Dubai there are two concessionary areas, the one on shore and the other off shore, but the ownership of these concessions has run a somewhat chequered course, with numerous changes in the participating companies and in the proportions of their holdings. Briefly, the history of ownership has been as follows. In April 1963 the Continental Oil Company (Conoco) acquired the onshore concession and set up the Dubai Petroleum Company (DPC) to operate the concession. In the same year DPC acquired for Conoco a half-share in the offshore concession held by Dubai Marine Areas Ltd (DUMA). The remaining half-share was retained by BP, which held a two-thirds interest in it, and the Compagnie Française des Pétroles, which retained the other third. In the following year, DPC granted a share in the onshore concession to Deutsche Erdöl AG (DEA) and to the Sun Oil Company. It also granted participations in its half-share of the offshore concession to DEA (10 per cent) and to Sun Oil (5 per cent).

During 1969 BP retired from participation in the Dubai offshore concession, selling its interest to the French company, which in turn sold half of its interest in DUMA to Hispanoil, a Spanish firm. The frequent changes in ownership are all very confusing and complicated but the position of the offshore concession reached in 1969, when oil began to flow, can best be shown in a tabular statement as given below.

Owning Company	Share of ownership
Dubai Marine Areas Ltd (half owned by CFP and half by Hispanoil)	50%
Dubai Petroleum Co (the operating company)	35%
Deutsche Erdöl AG	10%
Dubai Sun Oil Co	5%

The search for oil in Dubai began in earnest in 1963 but did not have a very propitious start, as the two wells drilled on land to depths respectively of 15,401 feet and 10,200 feet were unsuccessful and had to be abandoned. A third well drilled, this time off shore, also had to be abandoned after reaching a depth of over 12,000 feet. These failures occurred in 1964. In 1965, DPC concentrated its efforts on the offshore concession and in 1966 hired the *Glomer Tasman* to drill in what was considered to be a promising area some sixty miles from land. Early in June 1966 it was announced that oil had been found at a depth of 7,600 feet in what is now known as the Fateh Field. Two weeks later a second producing zone was discovered at 8,300 feet. Two further wells were then drilled which confirmed that commercial quantities of oil existed in the field.

Production from the Fateh Field, so named by the Ruler, Shaikh Rashid, and meaning "good fortune", began on 6 September 1969, and on 22 September the *Ocean Lancer*, a 26,000-ton tanker, moored in the Fateh Field and loaded 180,000 barrels of crude oil, Dubai's first shipment, which was dispatched to a refinery in England. In 1972 production amounted to 153,000 barrels a day, in 1973 to 220,000 barrels a day, and in 1974 to 310,000.

Shipment of oil from the field presented difficulties owing to its distance from the shore and the shallowness of the coastal waters. To surmount the difficulties an ingenious system of oil-storage has been adopted. An under-water storage tank was assembled on the shore and towed to its location sixty-five miles out in the Gulf. The tank is a circular, dome-shaped unit, 205 feet high and 270 feet in diameter, shaped like an inverted funnel. It has a capacity of half a million barrels of oil and is securely anchored to the sea-bed, 155 feet under water. The advantage claimed for this under-water storage system is that it eliminated the construction of many miles of pipe-line, the building of ports and harbours, and the setting-up of a tank farm on shore. As only the tip of the funnel projects out of the sea, there is little interference with shipping movements in the area. Tankers, even those of the super-tanker class, can tie up nearby and easily load up with crude oil even during periods of relatively bad weather.

The unit operates on the water–oil displacement system. Oil and water have different densities and do not mix. As crude oil is pumped into the tank from the wells, it forces the water out. Then, as a tanker is loaded, the reverse process takes place, with water flowing into the tank to replace the oil that is pumped out.

The tank, named Khazzan ("storage") Dubai I, was towed out to the field in August 1969, having been made buoyant by being filled with compressed air. So successful has been this unique storage system that a second tank was launched on 2 June 1972, and a third has now been built.

In addition to the submerged tank, there is also a floating tanker storage system. To provide this, two tanker bodies were rebuilt into a couple of floating storage vessels with a combined capacity of 645,000 barrels. These floating storage vessels are fully automated and are fed with crude oil from the wells through their bottoms, by means of a flexible hose which allows the vessels to move naturally at their moorings.

Ownership of the oil and gas fields within Dubai's territory has now been assumed by the Government under an agreement with the existing oil companies signed in July 1975. The companies, which received compensation amounting to $110 million for their assets, continue to operate the fields and market the oil.

OIL IN SHARJAH

Searching for oil in Sharjah went on for many years and there were many disappointments before success was achieved. Exploration began in 1962 when the John W. Mecon Company and the Pure Oil Company jointly obtained both the onshore and offshore concessions for Sharjah together with those for the smaller emirates of Ajman and Um al Quaiwain. Four offshore and two onshore wells were drilled but no commercial quantities of oil were found, though one of the wells on land yielded small quantities of oil. The two companies eventually relinquished their concessions in 1967. The three emirates then separately invited bids for their concessions. The Shell Oil Company secured the land concession in Sharjah but the offshore concession of 500,000 acres went to one of the smaller American oil companies, Buttes Gas and Oil of San Francisco; though Buttes acted as the operating company, it was associated with Crescent Petroleum, which was in turn associated with four other share-holding companies. Under the arrangement, Buttes came to own 35 per cent of the capital; Ashland Oil 25 per cent; Shell Oil 25 per cent; Kerr McGee 12·5 per cent and Juniper Petroleum 2·5 per cent. Two wells were drilled off Abu Musa Island, and drilling to between 13,000 and 14,000 feet under 200 feet of water found oil in sufficient quantities in October 1972 to confirm that a new field, named Mubarak Field, had been discovered, which would yield oil in commercial quantities. The oil has a low sulphur content which makes it readily marketable in countries which have become pollution-conscious.

A production platform was built to pipe oil from the wells for storage in a floating tanker-hulk, named *Baraka I*, of 82,000 tons capacity. This is connected to tanker-mooring facilities in 200 feet of water. Oil came on stream in June 1974 with an initial production of about 80,000 barrels a day.

The island of Abu Musa lies about 50 miles from the UAE coast, and political complications arose in connection with Sharjah's ownership of the oil field. Iran claimed suzerainty over the island when the British forces were leaving the Gulf in 1971 but the dispute over ownership was amicably settled by an agreement reached on 29 December 1971. Both countries will share oil revenues on a 50/50 basis within the 12 mile coastal limit after Sharjah's revenue from the oil field reaches £3 million sterling, but in the meantime Iran contracted to pay £1·5 million sterling annually. A dispute also arose between Crescent Petroleum of Sharjah and the Occidental Oil Company with its offshore rights in Um al Quaiwain and Ajman. Sharjah's 12 miles offshore claim was contested, but eventually in 1975 the dispute was settled by allowing Um al Quaiwain a 30 per cent share in Sharjah's oil receipts from the Abu Musa Field.

Exploitation of the new oilfield has brought a dramatic change in fortune for the three hundred inhabitants of Abu Musa, who previously had subsisted by fishing, collecting turtle eggs, or working in the red oxide mines. But even more important has been the great stimulus which oil discovery has given to the economy of mainland Sharjah. This is particularly evident in the port, which has become a hive of intense activity as supplies and materials arrive for shipping to the oil field.

Encouraged by the successful exploitation of the Mubarak Field, hopes have grown that further oil fields are waiting to be discovered. In mid-1974 drilling started in a new offshore concession granted to Crystal Oil Company of the USA. About the same time, another agreement was signed with Reserve Oil and Gas Company, also of the USA, for exploration in territorial waters and the continental shelf off Sharjah's eastern region. This company also signed a similar agreement with Fujairah.

SEARCHING FOR OIL IN THE NORTHERN EMIRATES

Though intensive searches for oil have been made in Ajman, Um al Quaiwain, Ras al Khaimah and Fujairah, no success has as yet been attained in finding oil in commercial quantities.

In Ras al Khaimah a concession was awarded in 1964 for development on land and off shore to the Ras al Khaimah Petroleum Company, which was jointly owned by the Union Oil Company of California (80 per cent) and the South Natural Gas Company (20 per cent). Seismic surveys were carried out and drilling began in 1966 but without success. In 1967 South Natural Gas ceded its share to its partner, and so Union Oil of California became the sole owner of the Ras al Khaimah Petroleum Company. Four offshore wells were drilled and though these had to be abandoned, some small traces of oil had appeared which encouraged the company to secure the use of one of the largest offshore drilling rigs constructed up to that date, namely the *Bull Run*. The rig was towed by two tugs all the way from Texas and arrived at Ras al Khaimah in the summer of 1970 to begin drilling there.

Union Oil of California eventually gave up the struggle to find oil, and was succeeded in July 1973 by three other companies encouraged by higher oil prices to continue the search. These were a Dutch company, Vitol Exploration, Peninsular Petroleum and Norsk Hydro. Vitol, which holds an offshore concession, started exploration in 1973 and has expressed hopes of success in the near future.

Fujairah, apt to be the forgotten state of Trucial Oman, did not attract much attention from the oil companies and did not seem to offer much possibility of finding oil, especially as the continental shelf is very narrow off the Batinah Coast. In 1967, however, a concession carrying both oil and mineral rights was negotiated with a German company, Bomin Bochumer Mineralgesellschaft. The concession

NATURAL GAS IN ABU DHABI

In Abu Dhabi, as elsewhere in the Gulf, opportunities for the utilization of associated gases from the oil-fields have been limited, as there are no large consuming centres nearby to provide a market. Some of the gas has been piped to Abu Dhabi Town to provide fuel for the electric generating and desalination plants. New industries such as the cement works in Al Ain or the proposed steel mill may provide further uses, but even with these new industries the demand would be far less than the available supplies, as it is estimated that the oil-fields could produce between one and two billion cubic feet of gas daily from associated gases alone; that is apart from any new independent gas-fields that might be developed. Thus, utilization of natural gas that is at present flared, or the exploitation of the independent gas-fields require the development of liquefaction plants.

The liquefied natural gas (LNG) plant on Das Island is the first of its kind to be built in the Arabian Gulf. Its foundation stone was laid by Sheikh Zaid on 4 December 1973, and the plant should be completed in 1976. It covers one third of the island, which itself has an area of approximately one square mile. Processing associated gas at present flared at the off-shore fields, it will produce annually up to two million tons of LNG and one million tons of liquefied petroleum gas (LPG). In addition, up to 220 thousand tons per annum of light distillate and 250 tons of flaked sulphur will be produced.

Chapter 6

Agriculture

In most of the developing countries of the world, agriculture is the mainstay of their economies, but in the Gulf agriculture occupies a minor role, owing to the scarcity of water. The cereal field crops such as wheat, barley, or rice are practically unknown, though tradition has it that at one time such crops were extensively grown, for example in certain parts of the mountain area. The cultivated, irrigated lands are under date palms, vegetables, fruit, and alfalfa (lucerne). Alfalfa, used as a fodder for animals, can be cultivated intensively, and it is not unknown for ten to twelve cuttings to be made in a year. Annual yields of up to eighty tons per acre have been reported, and the plants are very tolerant of a fairly high degree of salinity. It is important as a cash crop for sale in the market and for growers feeding their own animals. It is not, however, as rewarding financially to the farmers as the growing of vegetables or fruit by modern techniques.

Agriculture in the Federation is confined very largely to a few oases, or to specially favoured localities such as parts of Ras al Khaimah or of the Batinah Coast. Abu Dhabi, by far the largest of the emirates in area, is mainly desert or scrub, except in its Eastern Province of Al Ain, near a mountain range which provides such plentiful supplies of fresh water that a few years ago Abu Dhabi Town could rely upon them for all its requirements. The source is at As Sadd, about twenty-one kilometres from Al Ain Town at a point near the road between Al Ain and Abu Dhabi, and was connected by two pipe-lines, 130 kilometres in length, to Abu Dhabi Town. The whole supply of domestic water in Abu Dhabi Town is now produced by distillation, leaving Al Ain's water to be utilized solely in the Eastern Province. Sea-water distillation, though possible and economic for domestic water supplies, is as yet too expensive a process for commercial agriculture.

Historically and geographically, the Al Ain Oasis is of considerable importance, as it forms a meeting place of trades routes in south-east Arabia. It was inhabited by Omani tribes for centuries before the coming of Islam, its ancient name being

Towwam. Evidence provided by recently excavated archaeological sites shows indeed that it was settled as far back as the third millennium BC. In 1955 the Buraimi oasis was the subject of an ownership dispute when Saudi Arabia claimed suzerainty, though several hundred miles separate it from the nearest settled part of Saudi Arabia. The Omani village of Hamara was occupied for a time, but both Abu Dhabi and Oman, with the support of the British government, strongly opposed the claim. Eventually the dispute was patched up and remained quiescent until 1974, when Saudi Arabia relinquished her claim, obtaining in return a small wedge of territory adjoining Qatar and giving Saudi Arabia an outlet to the Gulf. In addition, the southern boundary was readjusted in Saudi Arabia's favour.

In the recent past, however different it may have been centuries ago, the Al Ain Oasis produced little else than dates and alfalfa, though in Buraimi Village there are many well-established gardens with fruit trees sheltered by date palms. Now the trend is towards diversification of agricultural production, with special emphasis on vegetable crops and certain kinds of fruit. In the Al Ain villages about 10 per cent of the working population in 1968 was engaged in farming, but since then the number of farms and farm workers has steadily increased. Now about 800 persons find employment in agriculture, an increase of more than 20 per cent over 1968.

THE LIWA OASIS

The Liwa Oasis ("the wide valley") is very different. Approaching the Liwa by air, one flies for mile after mile over irregular sand dunes, many looking like gigantic golf-course bunkers. In places the sands are of a pinkish colour and hardly a track is to be seen among them, still less any roads. The first settlements to be approached are very small, consisting of only a few houses and far apart from other habitations. Further into the oasis, the settlements are closer and more concentrated with groups of perhaps twenty to thirty houses. All the houses are of *barasti* type, constructed from date-palm fronds and branches, and grouped in twos, threes, or fours surrounded by a high *barasti* fence designed to keep out the shifting sands. The houses are invariably built at the top or very near the top of the sand dune, so as to obtain the advantage of any cooling breeze that may blow. They are surprisingly cool considering the hot climate and lack of shade from trees. "Each building is rectangular, about 12 feet wide and up to 30 feet long, the length being determined by the size of the palm-trunks used as beams. There are no windows but there is a door (made of palm frond mats) in the centre of each of the ends. When the doors are closed the whole building presents a uniform box-like appearance."[1]

The palm trees which thrive in the area are grown on the lower slopes of the dunes below the houses or in hollows between the dunes. The date gardens are

[1] Dr Frauk Heard-Bey, "Development Anomalies in the Bedouin Oasis of Al-Liwa", *Asian Affairs*, Vol. 61, October 1974. The article contains a valuable account of the oasis with much information not available elsewhere.

well arranged, with their trees systematically planted in regular formation and irrigated. No evidence, however, is to be seen of any green vegetation around the homesteads, though in the hollows below the date gardens desert vegetation is found. Generally this vegetation is very sparse but in some places it is relatively abundant, suggesting the availability of water supplies for further agricultural development. It is, however, as yet uncertain how far supplies of good water will enable this development to proceed. At present, cultivation in the Liwa is almost exclusively confined to the growing of date palms, but a beginning is being made in the growing of vegetables. Development depends largely on improvement in communications, and roads are now being planned to link the Liwa with Tarif.

The inhabitants of the Liwa are not as settled as those in many other parts of Abu Dhabi, and the resident population tends to fluctuate with the seasons. Some of the villagers migrate with their flocks and herds for the winter grazings but return for the summer months when the desert is bare. Others may move to the coast or to the islands for the fishing season. At a peak, it would appear that about 3,000 persons inhabit the oasis, but at other times there may be considerably fewer than 2,000. Development of the Liwa is still at the stage of making the best use of known resources. Should hydrological surveys disclose the presence of new sources of water and if roads are built, then new life could be instilled into the area. It may be, however, that the younger people will be attracted to the towns and reject the austere conditions of life in the oasis.

THE EXPERIMENTAL FARM

Much of the progress in farming achieved in Abu Dhabi over the past five or six years has been due to the activities of the Department of Agriculture, which started operations in 1967 with headquarters at Al Ain, the obvious centre for its activities. An experimental farm was established in the autumn of 1968 with a threefold aim: (1) to find what varieties of plants were best suited to the climatic and other conditions prevailing in Al Ain and elsewhere in the emirate; (2) to develop the most suitable strains of seed for subsequent distribution to farmers; (3) to develop demonstration plots so that farmers can be shown good methods of cultivation.

As a starting-point, the management of the farm sought information about possible new crops and plant varieties from countries such as Iraq, Saudi Arabia, and Jordan, where climatic conditions are fairly similar to those of Abu Dhabi. It was found that many vegetables new to the area were easily acclimatized, but that fruit-tree cultivation was more difficult as only certain species can be successfully grown in Abu Dhabi. Among cash crops, strawberries and flowers have been notably successful.

Seeds, seedlings, and plants are made available by the experimental farm free of cost to all those who may need them, including those persons whose interest is in their own private garden.

The experimental farm now covers an area of 800 donums (200 acres) and there are four agricultural extension centres which demonstrate good methods of cultivation and which help the farmers to introduce new crops.

Poultry farming, however, which obviously has good prospects in Abu Dhabi, is being left to private enterprise as it is not in need of subsidies or of direct government help.

Considerable attention is now being given to forestry, and 1,625 acres have been planted with trees along the highway between Al Ain and Abu Dhabi Town. Another 2,375 acres are to be planted in other areas such as the oil centres of Tarif and Jebel Dhanna, and alongside the new road to Dubai. The aim is to transform a not inconsiderable part of the landscape in selected areas of Abu Dhabi from sandy, wind-blown desert to green forest, thereby greatly increasing amenities, improving the climate, reducing the severity of dust storms, and preventing soil erosion. Several varieties of trees have been selected as suitable to local conditions, and already half a million tree seedlings have been distributed.

The supply of irrigation water, rather than land area and suitability of soil, is the limiting factor to the development of agriculture. It is estimated, however, that in Al Ain there is enough water available to irrigate an area of 7,500 acres.

The experimental farm is concerned not only to introduce new crops and extend the area of cultivation but also to help the farmers protect their growing crops from the ravages of harmful pests. Spraying of crops began in 1968 and has now been developed to the stage where the Department of Agriculture has its own aeroplane specially suited and equipped for crop spraying.

Strenuous efforts are being made by the department not only to improve existing farms and farming methods but also to encourage the establishment of new farms. Local nationals, including Bedouin pastoralists who desire to become arable farmers, are given seven donums (1¾ acres) of horticultural land free of all cost and are set up with the necessary farm machinery and pumps. They are also provided with seeds, seedlings, and all essential items. To help them to get established on their farms and to tide them over the period before the farm can be made remunerative, they are given a monthly maintenance grant of DH 300 for two years. Already about 600 farms have been established. It is not easy, however, to persuade Bedouins, accustomed in the past to a nomadic way of life tending flocks of sheep and goats and herds of camels, to become arable farmers or market gardeners. The older men, it has been found, are often willing to settle to farming, but the younger men tend to be attracted by the lure of the towns.

In Dubai, an experimental farm was started in the autumn of 1974 at Rawaya.

THE GRAZING GROUNDS OF ABU DHABI

In Abu Dhabi there has never been as clear a demarcation as elsewhere in Arabia between the settled communities and the nomad Bedouin. There was much overlapping and the tribes often spent only part of the year in the desert tending their animals. In the emirate there are several good grazing areas including Al Dhafra, Bainunah and Al Hamra. Al Dhafra is located in the centre of the state and provides grazing grounds for the nomads. Grazing is particularly good in Bainunah, which stretches between the middle part of Abu Dhabi's coastline and the north-west part of Al Dhafra, extending inland for about forty miles. This area is one of undulating sand dunes but has sufficient water, though it is somewhat brackish, for the winter grazing of the nomads' herds.

Further east the dunes become higher and larger as one recedes from the coast. Still further east, between the coast and the Liwa, there are some sweet-water wells, and clumps of date palm trees are to be found in the hollows. North and somewhat east of the Liwa there is an area of wide sandy plains called Ramlat Al Hamra, which is broken by salt flats, valleys, and a few hills. The grazing is good and fresh-water wells are fairly numerous. Beyond there lies a sinister and dangerous region of quicksands known as Um al Semim, "the mother of poison".

South of the Liwa there is an area called Batin, where there are high sand dunes. The wells are salty so the area is practically uninhabited, though camels can survive there on salt bushes, which are sufficiently plentiful to provide them with food. Still further south lies Kidan, where the sand dunes are white or golden, in contrast with the red sands of the Rub al Khali desert behind them.

The pastures of Al Khatan lie mainly west of Al Ain, with the road to Abu Dhabi Town passing through.

AGRICULTURE IN RAS AL KHAIMAH

Ras al Khaimah, alone among the six states of the Federation which border the Arabian Gulf, has considerable possibilities for agricultural development. Rainfall exceeds that of the other emirates, with an annual average of 150 millimetres (six inches), and in a good rain-year may exceed 200 millimetres (eight inches). A higher proportion of the population is engaged in agriculture than in the other states, and a feature of the population distribution is the large number of villages both along the coast and inland. Elsewhere in the Federation, with a few exceptions such as Al Ain, villages are few and far between.

In Ras al Khaimah good arable land is to be found along the coast and in the foothills of the mountains, where ample supplies of water from rain or underground sources are available. The land looks green and pleasant as there are numerous well-cultivated gardens, and many trees and shrubs are to be seen growing wild.

In the northern section of Ras al Khaimah, cultivable agricultural land extends from Sha'am to Digdagga, where the experimental farm is located. The southern section of the emirate, which is cut off from the northern part by a strip of territory belonging to Fujairah, is even more predominantly agricultural, and there are many villages, notably Al Darah, Darq, Qor, and Mania, where farming is a thriving occupation. This southern section is completely landlocked by Oman, Sharjah, Fujairah, and Dubai. It is the centre of an intricate mosaic of territorial diversity which complicates any attempt at a clear geographical description of the area.

The town of Ras al Khaimah and the surrounding district contain numerous date gardens and fruit and vegetable farms. A great variety of crops are cultivated.

Among the fruits there are dates, bananas, plantains, oranges and lemons, figs, grapes, and pawpaws, as well as varieties less well known in the Federation such as mulberries, mangoes, pomegranates, and strawberries. The vegetables success-fully grown include both winter and summer varieties and among them may be mentioned tomato, egg-plant, marrow, cabbage, cauliflower, cucumber, onion, radish, turnip, and parsley. Alfalfa is grown for animal fodder. Considerable quantities of fruit and vegetables are exported to Dubai, Sharjah, and as far away as Abu Dhabi. This export has considerably increased in recent years as a result of the completion of a first-class metalled road to Sharjah and Dubai. Many lorries now go direct to Abu Dhabi with dates and vegetable produce. In 1971 these lorries numbered 1,490, showing an almost ten-fold increase over previous years. In ad-dition to the production of fruit and vegetables, a certain amount of good-quality cream cheese is made. Tobacco is also cultivated in small quantities for local con-sumption. This is usually smoked in tiny pipes, from which the smoker takes only one puff each time it is filled.

South-east of the town of Ras al Khaimah there are many agricultural holdings in a tract of land known as the Jiri. In this area there are several hot mineral-water springs much reputed locally for their curative properties; that at Khatt, about twenty-five kilometres south of the town, being especially famed. This source has obviously been held in high esteem from very early times, as nearby there was an ancient temple with a huge idol. The temple was demolished by Wahabis years ago, but the ruins are still there.

Ras al Khaimah is held in some regard for holiday residences, especially since communications have been so vastly improved by the construction of roads. Gulf shaikhs own farms and houses in such attractive spots as Al Kharran, Solhiya, Shamal, and Sha'am, as do rich merchants from Saudi Arabia, Kuwait, and Qatar. A hotel and a casino have been built on the outskirts of the town, which help to attract visitors, especially from Dubai.

Much of the credit for the diversification of fruit and vegetable cultivation must go to the Agricultural Trials Station at Digdagga. This was established in 1955 in a very modest way by Robin Huntingdon, who had formerly served as an officer with the Trucial Oman Levies. After retiring from the army and after a short period of watercress farming in England, he returned to Ras al Khaimah with the somewhat visionary aim of establishing a kind of Owenite community centre where activities would include not only improved and diversified agriculture but also rural crafts such as pottery and weaving, as well as educational facilities. The ideal settlement which he envisaged never came to full fruition, but this dedicated pioneer, starting with only two *barasti* huts, was able to initiate and organize a most valuable experimental farm and agricultural school situated some twelve miles from the town of Ras al Khaimah, reached then through a roadless red earth dis-trict, dotted with wild vegetation and trees.

The testing of varieties of vegetables and fruit trees has continued on the farm ever since 1955, and the centre has developed steadily, with financial assistance from the British government and from the Trucial States Development Office. Now it has its own permanent offices, a veterinary clinic, an agricultural school, a mechanics' workshop, poultry houses, and a fine herd of pedigree Friesian cattle. It manages three farms which cultivate plants and grow seedlings for distribution, as well as serving as experimental stations and demonstration plots. These are situated at Digdagga (the parent farm of sixty acres), Falaj al Muallah (five acres), and Kalba (seven acres). In addition there is at Meleiha an area of 300 acres which has been acquired for development as a unit, utilizing modern methods of irrigation. The whole area is eventually to be parcelled out among local farmers, and already the network of irrigation canals has been completed over the whole 300 acres.

The agricultural school at Digdagga is unique in the Federation as being the only specialized agricultural school. It accepts students from all the states of the Federation for a three-year course in theoretical and practical agricultural studies, provided they have completed a minimum of six years' elementary education. In 1969, an adult education programme was also initiated by the school, and in the first year of this scheme fifteen adult students attended the evening classes, which covered agriculture, language, and general knowledge.

The trials section experiments with the growing of plants new to the area and with new strains of existing varieties. Starting with the introduction of red radish and American cabbage by Huntingdon, many new crops have been introduced over the years. The agricultural extension service provided by the farm assists farmers in their choice of crops and advises them on methods of cultivation, including the use of fertilizers.

The farm is making great efforts to improve local livestock through cross-breeding, and great hopes are entertained for the development of livestock and dairy farming in Ras al Khaimah and selected districts of other emirates. A valuable herd of thirty pure-bred Friesian cattle was imported from the United Kingdom a few years ago and a complete pasteurization plant has been set up to treat milk in commercial quantities for marketing in the Federation. Special attention is being given to the housing, care, and feeding of the herd so as to determine the optimum conditions for such animals in the area. This work is of great importance because the general standard of livestock in the Federation is poor. As Dr Faulkner of the Food and Agriculture Organization (FAO) stated in 1970 in his report on Animal Husbandry in the Northern Trucial States: "Animal production is at present mainly a Bedouin activity. Unknown numbers of adaptable but low-producing sheep, goats, cattle and camels, with the goat predominating, are herded on a semi-nomadic basis in this region. Conditions for livestock generally, except where irrigated agriculture is undertaken, are adverse in the extreme. Supplementary feeding is not commonly practised. Infectious pleuro-pneumonia is rife throughout the goat population of the region and presents a difficult problem. Tick-borne diseases and foot-and-mouth disease will present severe problems in cattle production with the introduction of exotic, high-yielding stock. Similar problems will arise in poultry production as flocks increase in numbers."

Because of the risks from tick-borne and other diseases, farmers are being advised to confine their cattle to pens, particularly in towns and villages. Animals allowed to roam freely are liable to serious risks, for example from ticks, which are so numerous as to cover the legs of the animals entirely. The experts at Dig-dagga say that they do not mind if their animals get one or two bites, as this may serve as a kind of inoculation, but serious infection kills an animal.

The government of Ras al Khaimah is encouraging its nationals to become farmers by giving them plots of land averaging four acres in extent if they do not already own land of their own. This encouragement is commendable because the trend in recent years has been for labour to find employment in government service or in private trade rather than in agriculture or fishing. Large numbers of the in-habitants of Ras al Khaimah have migrated to Abu Dhabi or to Dubai, where opportunities of employment are greater. In order to prevent the land being taken over by speculators who might hold out for higher prices, those granted a plot of land are required to develop the allotment within a period of five years.

Though most of the fruit gardens and other agricultural holdings are small, there are several large private farms run on modern lines. Poultry-farming especi-ally lends itself to such larger units, and under careful management can be very successful in a sub-tropical climate. The birds reared and the eggs produced com-pare very favourably with those of poultry farms in the temperate climates of European countries. This need not cause any surprise, for the hen, after all, was not indigenous to Europe, but was imported from warmer climates long ago. The varieties bred for temperate climates and for conditions in Europe may not be the best suited to sub-tropical conditions, and the whole science and practice of poultry-farming in warmer climates require examination and research. The birds need to be given more space, and the building should be higher than is usual in Europe, where temperatures are so much lower. Special attention is required to hygiene, and casual visitors should be discouraged from moving around the hen-houses lest infection should be carried on footwear or clothing. There is a big demand for fresh chicken and fresh eggs in the Federation, and already two large intensive poultry farms have been established on the outskirts of Dubai, and another just outside the town of Al Ain in Abu Dhabi.

UNDERGROUND WATER SUPPLIES IN THE FEDERATION

There are no rivers or lakes in the United Arab Emirates, and all supplies of water, other than from sea-water distillation, are obtained from wells or brought in underground canals from the mountains. Within the region there are literally thousands of wells. Many are very ancient and have been used by nomadic tribes from time out of mind. Some few yield sweet water, but mostly the water is of varying degrees of brackishness. Many of the wells have been neglected, and that division of the Trucial States Development Office which dealt with water in the northern states therefore embarked on a regular programme of clearing out the old wells and digging new. Between 1969 and 1971 more than 160 wells were drilled, many of them equipped with pumps. In Abu Dhabi, also, wells have been cleaned out, cemented where necessary, and provided with pumps.

In the northern states, many villages have suffered severely during periods of drought from a reduction of water supply or even from a total loss of their supply, causing not only personal hardship but also loss of livelihood through the failure of their crops.

THE AFLAJ, OR UNDERGROUND WATER CANALS

A particularly interesting feature of agriculture in the Federation is the *falaj* (plural *aflaj*) or underground water canal, which taps a source of water in the hills or mountains and brings the water through gently sloping tunnels to the farms, sometimes over distances of twenty miles or more. In places they may be as deep as forty feet below the surface. Many of the *aflaj* are of considerable antiquity, and their constructors displayed great ingenuity and a high degree of technical expertise both in locating sources of water underground and in constructing the tunnels. *Aflaj* are to be found in many parts of the Federation, in the Al Ain Oasis, in Fujairah, Dubai, Sharjah, and Ajman. They probably originated in Persia, where they are known as *qanat*, and where certain tribes or families were specially and traditionally skilled in their construction and maintenance and possessed an almost uncanny knowledge of where sources of water could be found. The Persian techniques spread over a wide part of Arabia, and channels built originally by Persians are to be found not only in the Federation, but also in Oman, Bahrain, and Iraq, adapted where necessary to the conditions of the district.

In the Federation, the tunnels start at a source in the hills where water is held in permeable rock overlying a stratum of impervious rock and can be drained off into the tunnel. These tunnels are normally about five feet square, that is, just wide enough and high enough for a man to work inside them. The method of construction was to dig vertical shafts at regular intervals along the proposed line of route and then to excavate between them. The shafts provided fresh air for the workers and allowed the spoil to be removed. The route followed by the underground canals can often be easily followed as it is marked by a line of mounds formed by the debris excavated through the shafts. When viewed from the air they resemble a regular series of huge mole-hills. When the canal was completed, the source was opened and the water flowed down the gently sloping channels. Thereafter the shafts served to provide access for workers engaged in maintaining and repairing the canals and as a means of disposing of silt and refuse which might block the canal. Where water was required en route, it was raised to the surface by buckets, or nowadays by pumps. Some of these wells tapping the water supply are of considerable depth; one may be seen on the experimental farm at Al Ain. Where the land sloped sufficiently but not too greatly, the canals appeared at the surface; an example of this can be found only a short distance from the new Hilton Hotel in Al Ain.

The tunnels and the wells are generally solidly constructed and it is a tribute to the ingenuity and skill of the *aflaj* builders that today channels perhaps centuries old which had fallen into decay and disuse are being cleared out and repaired to provide life-giving water for a revived agriculture. The Trucial States Development Council was very active in resuscitating the *aflaj*. Their biggest project of this kind was the cleaning and repair of an extensive system at Hatta in Dubai, which provides the main source of water for the village. The channel was roofed and the source extended. Elsewhere repairs to *aflaj* have been carried out at Masfut (Ajman), Saqamqam (Fujairah), Fili (Sharjah), and Ziht (Fujairah). Among other such works there may be mentioned those at Falaj Lisaili and Falaj Habbab, which were cleared and roofed with reinforced concrete slabs. In Abu Dhabi, much work has been done by the government to improve the *aflaj* in Al Ain, including the concreting of the channels where they reach the surface to provide watering places for animals and washing facilities.

ARID-ZONE TECHNOLOGY

Scarcity of water and increasing salinity pose a challenge to agricultural scientists and governments in all arid areas of the world. Arid-zone technology, though not yet attracting the attention it deserves, is now making definite progress.

In Abu Dhabi, outside the oases, the harsh climate and the lack of water present apparently almost insoluble problems for agriculture. Of outstanding interest therefore is the project of the Arid Lands Research Centre on Sadiyat Island. This scheme of controlled environmental agriculture is supplementary but in complete contrast to the projects for the renewal of the ancient system of *aflaj*. The one rests on the application of modern science and technology, the other on the wisdom of the past. The simplest form of controlling environment for agriculture is the green-house, but the project now operative on Sadiyat Island takes it a stage further into the technological age. This project is an integrated complex for the generation of electrical energy, for the de-salination of sea-water, and for food production. Waste heat from the engines which drive the generators is used to de-salt sea-water, and the fresh water so obtained is utilized for the irrigation of vegetables planted inside greenhouses of air-inflated plastic material. The system was devised by the Environmental Research Laboratory of the University of Arizona, which specializes in arid-zone technology, and was first tried out at Puerto Penasco in Mexico, which has a climate not very dissimilar to that of the Trucial Coast. The plant in Abu Dhabi, however, is much larger, and in the summer of 1972 was producing one ton a day of vegetables such as tomatoes, cucumbers, green beans, peppers, lettuces, cabbages, and spinach, which are marketed in Abu Dhabi Town.

In the plastic greenhouses, both irrigation and atmospheric conditions are closely controlled. The water from the de-salination plant is enriched with plant nutrients appropriate to the requirements of the particular crops being grown. Different types of irrigation are or will be used, depending on such factors as the species or the nature of the crop. One method is the use of above-ground sprinklers which emit a fine spray over the growing area. This is suited to closely spaced crops such as radishes. Another method is to water each plant individually from a network of very small plastic tubes. The third method depends on the release of water in small droplets at soil level. This is a method which has been found very successful elsewhere in Abu Dhabi for watering young trees. In all three systems, the water is applied as needed, with up to four applications a day. Only enough water is added at a time to moisten the sand beds to the depth of root penetration. The mistake made in many parts of the Middle East which follow traditional methods of furrow or flood irrigation is to apply too much water when water is available. This may do as much harm as good by increasing salinity, and it is wasteful of scarce supplies.

The atmosphere in the pressure-inflated greenhouses is kept at high humidity, approaching 100 per cent at ambient temperatures, and to prevent loss of humidity entrance into the greenhouses is through an air-lock. At one end of the greenhouse sea-water is sprayed through a stack of corrugated asbestos to meet a current of air passing in the opposite direction. The moistened air-current is then directed to flow the length of the greenhouse and back again for more moisture. The water picked up by the air is salt-free, just as the sun evaporates salt-free water from the oceans. Within the greenhouse the air cycle is virtually a closed one, and sweeps through the spraying column every two minutes, while the spent sea-water flows back to the Gulf. Air velocity prevents stagnation on the leaf surface of the plants, and, to prevent depletion of the carbon dioxide level by photosynthesizing plants, carbon dioxide is added to the air. At Puerto Penasco the required supplies of carbon dioxide are obtained from the diesel engine exhausts—a nice example of integrated planning.

In another venture in Abu Dhabi, a horticultural project has been initiated in a desert region 125 miles inland at Mazaid. This will cover 15 acres, and plastic globes are being employed to provide a controlled environment.

AGRICULTURE ON THE BATINAH COAST

Fujairah is the only state of the Federation located entirely on the Batinah Coast of the Gulf of Oman, but there are a number of dependencies belonging to Sharjah situated on this coast, including Kalba, Khor Fakkan, and Dibba, the last named being itself divided into two zones, one belonging to Sharjah and the other, called Husn, to Fujairah. Along the Batinah Coast, there runs a narrow strip of fertile land, backed by hills and mountains where there are also some fertile areas of land. The village of Khor Fakkan in particular is green and fertile, attractively situated in a bay with many gardens, and dominated by high mountains rising several thousand feet. The main activities of the region are agriculture and fishing. In Fujairah two-thirds of the working population are farmers and a further 13 per cent are fishermen. The main agricultural products are dates, fruit, and vegetables, but these are consumed locally except for a small export of dried lemons and tobacco. The coastal plain varies in width from about as little as one mile at the narrowest to as much as twenty miles at its widest, and sweeps round in a great arc, embellished with an almost continuous though narrow belt of date palms, gardens, and villages. Though there are many gardens, agriculture has fallen behind what it once was, but it can be expected that the completion of the trans-peninsular road through the Wadi Siji and the Wadi Ham will greatly stimulate agriculture by providing easy access to the markets of the Arabian Gulf Coast. The old route was very rough, and in places was merely a wadi bed with large stones and boulders to be negotiated only in four-wheel-drive vehicles.

AGRICULTURE IN THE OTHER STATES

Agricultural activities in Sharjah are concentrated largely in her dependencies, but only about 1,400 persons work in agriculture, which is less than half the number in Ras al Khaimah.

In the remaining states, namely Dubai, Ajman, and Um al Quaiwain, agricultural activity is relatively unimportant. In Dubai, agriculture accounts for only a little more than 2 per cent of the total labour force, and the whole economy of Dubai is slanted towards trade and commerce. In Ajman and Um al Quaiwain, fishing is more important than agriculture. In Ajman, not many more than 100 workers are employed in agriculture; three times that number are fishermen. In Um al Quaiwain, some 200, or 16 per cent, work in agriculture; 30 per cent are fishermen.

FOOD PREFERENCES

The emirates are large importers of foodstuffs and other agricultural products and the total annual value of retained food imports is approximately BD 20 million, that is, some DH 700 per head of the population per annum. There is a small amount of inter-regional trade in dried fish, dates, live animals, and fruit and vegetables from Ras al Khaimah, mainly to Dubai and Sharjah, and increasingly to Abu Dhabi. Export outside the Federation is very small, consisting of some dried fish and tiny quantities of such items as dried lemons.

Patterns of food consumption, standards of living, and food preferences vary between the national groups and between income groups. Out of the total population of the Federation as a whole, about one-third are expatriates. The largest expatriate groups are not Arab or European, but Iranian, Pakistani, and Indian, in that order. Their food consumption patterns are oriental rather than western, and of the low-cost type. It is not surprising therefore that the preferred cereal is rice. Indians have a somewhat higher purchasing power than, say, the Iranians, and they show a certain partiality for spices. Tinned and frozen foodstuffs are in demand by western expatriates and by some of the other higher-income groups, but the market is limited and the number of persons in the western group is only about 5,000. The demand for high-quality foodstuffs, however, is augmented by the international hotels of Abu Dhabi, Dubai and Sharjah, which during the cooler months of the year are usually fully booked.

Chapter 7

Pearling, Fishing, and Seafaring

Pearling, fishing, and seafaring have been the main occupations of the inhabitants of the Gulf coast for centuries. Pearling reached its zenith in the decades immediately preceding the First World War, when merchants from Paris and India visited the Gulf during the pearling season and eagerly sought the best specimens for their rich clients at home. In the 1930s, however, the industry practically collapsed owing to competition from Japanese cultured pearls and the depression in world trade. The industry never recovered from these disasters and the Gulf states sank into poverty. A hundred years before, it would appear that a total of more than 3,000 boats took part in pearling, the important centres being Kuwait, Bahrain, and the Trucial States. About 350 of the boats were from Abu Dhabi and about the same number were recorded for the combined fleets of Sharjah and Ras al Khaimah. Dubai also had a large fleet, numbering some 300 vessels. The industry continued to thrive and in 1905 the annual value of the pearl fishing in the Trucial States was estimated at a figure of eighty lakhs of rupees, that is, about £600,000. It was also estimated that over 22,000 men from the Trucial States went out to the pearl banks in well over a thousand boats.

The pearl merchants made large fortunes, and the Rulers who levied a tax on every boat relied on the industry as their main source of revenue. The divers and other members of the crews, however, did not fare so well, and many were hopelessly in debt to the merchants.

The pearling banks were open and free to all nationals of the area and were not regarded as being under the jurisdiction of any one shaikh. The inhabitants of countries other than those bordering on the Gulf were rigorously excluded from the pearl banks, and this traditional monopoly was confirmed by the British administration as part of the maritime peace enforced under the treaties.

The pearling expeditions were highly organized and the boats worked to a fixed schedule, all setting out on the same day and returning together as a group. It would have been very unusual for any boat or for any of the crews to visit their home port until the end of the season. This season, which was known as *Ghaus*, lasted approximately from 15 May to 15 September, and was so fixed because the divers could work only during the summer months, when the water was warm and the sea calm. Strict discipline was observed by the crews, who were expected to obey the captain of their boat in all matters, subject only to traditional customs and observances. This discipline was essential because pearling involved close team-work and co-operation. Duties were specialized and specific tasks were allotted to each man. The teams would comprise the captain, divers, haulers, assistants, and apprentices. Cooks, musicians, and prayer leaders were also included among the team.

The hauler, or *saib*, let the diver down to the sea-bed by a rope tied to a heavy stone. By holding on to this rope the diver was greatly helped in his dive, which was the most exhausting part of his task. The average diver could stay under water for about one minute, though experienced men might stay longer, perhaps even up to two minutes. Sometimes the divers operated at depths as great as ninety feet. The work of the diver was hard and exacting, with only a nose-peg of horn or wood to help him hold his breath. He ran a risk of being stung by blue jellyfish or sting-rays, or of having to meet the danger of an attack by a shark. To protect themselves from these hazards, it was customary for divers to work together in groups on the sea-bed. There was safety in numbers, as the predatory sharks or other dangerous fish would be frightened off more by a group than by an individual. Equipped with a knife to dislodge the oysters and to protect himself from attack, girdled by an apron with a large pocket to carry the oysters as they were gathered, the diver had to work hard and fast for the short time he was under water. The life of the diver was very much in the hands of the hauler, who had to remain on the alert so that he could haul the diver back immediately he felt a tug on the life-line. Between dives the divers took a short rest, sipping some coffee and perhaps eating one date. Food otherwise was not taken until after sunset, when the diving sessions ended.

The oysters were not opened immediately but were piled up on the deck to be opened later in a special session attended by all members of the crew. The Gulf oyster, it may be said, differs from the edible oysters known in Europe, and its only value apart from any pearls obtained would be for mother-of-pearl.

FISHERIES OF THE GULF

Though pearling has practically disappeared, fishing is still an important occupation in the Gulf, and the catches make an important contribution to the diet of many of the inhabitants of the area, especially as fish is an important source of animal protein. Some 9,000 persons are engaged in the fisheries, and large quantities of the fish caught in the Gulf over and above local requirements are dried and exported to South Asia or East Africa. The average consumption of fish in the Gulf states has been estimated to amount to about thirty kilos a head annually, which is considerably above the world average of ten kilos, though far below the per caput consumption in Japan and several other countries.

Many varieties of fish are caught in the waters of the Arabian Gulf, including kingfish, snapper, rock-cod, Red Sea bream, tuna, and crayfish. From September to March, fish are especially abundant in the Straits of Hormuz and for about 100 miles into the Gulf. During these months, there is a flow of colder water from the Gulf of Oman, which is more fertile and less saline than the Arabian Gulf, and this surge of water, which may reach four knots, carries with it large numbers of surface-swimming (pelagic) fish. Fishermen operating off Ras al Khaimah and Sha'am, and to a lesser extent in the waters between Dubai and Abu Dhabi, may then expect to obtain large catches of Spanish mackerel, sardines, and tuna. These pelagic fish are usually caught in "purse seine" nets, that is, in nets which have floats at the top and weights below, and which can be gathered in with ropes arranged like old-fashioned purse-strings. Other types of fish, which swim at lower levels, are caught by trawling the bottom of the sea-bed. Trawling, however, is not possible over about a third of the Gulf owing to shoals, reefs, and the uneven bottom. In such areas, and more especially around Bahrain, local fishermen use fish-traps, dredge-nets, or even hand-lines.

The fishing fleets of the Federation include many types of craft. At one extreme are diesel-engined ships of anything up to 150 h.p. and, at the other, primitive boats known as *Shasha*, which are built up from stems of palm trees. The *Shasha* are propelled by paddles or oars and have crews of three or four men. They are especially numerous in Fujairah but are also to be found in Sharjah. In between the largest and the smallest boats come various sized diesel-engined craft ranging from forty h.p. down to four h.p., including some with outboard motors. Several types of sailing vessels are also engaged in fishing, but they are all provided with paddles or oars to facilitate short-distance movements in the fishing areas or when becalmed. They include small and big *Shahufa*, the smaller being worked by three men, though the larger may have crews of as many as eight to fifteen men. Even larger crews are required to man the *Amla*, which depend on their oars rather than on their sail. Some of them are manned by crews numbering up to forty men. There are also canoe-type boats known as *Houris*, which are fitted with sails and paddles and are operated by three or four fishermen.

In Ajman, fishing is the most important occupation open to the inhabitants, and employs 27 per cent of the total working population. The fishing fleet of that shaikhdom includes forty-seven large vessels which operate all over the Gulf. Though the boats are of traditional design, they are very seaworthy and are fitted with powerful diesel engines. In Um al Quaiwain, fishing likewise is the predominant occupation, providing work for 460 fishermen, over 30 per cent of the working population. The Trucial States Development Office did much to develop the fisheries of this shaikhdom. A loan and grant scheme has also been introduced to help the fishermen by providing small diesel engines for their boats. One-third of the cost is paid for by the Ruler of Um al Quaiwain to the fishermen and the remaining two thirds are on loan from the Ruler to be repaid in instalments.

Fish caught in the Gulf are not frozen or processed but are either sold fresh in the market or else dried in the sun. In the past the fishermen would erect temporary huts or tents on the sea-shore during the months when they were drying the fish in the sun. The dried fish was sold by them to merchants who in turn either sold it in the interior, where it was highly regarded both for human consumption and as fodder for camels when grazing was not available, or else exported it either as food or as fertilizer. Dried fish is still of some importance and one can see fish being gutted and then dried in Ras al Khaimah, at Rams, and on the Batinah Coast. A fair amount is exported from Dubai and goes mainly to Ceylon and Saudi Arabia.

An unusual kind of dried fish is prepared from sharks, though only the tails and the fins are marketable. The fishermen of Ras al Khaimah are particularly skilled in catching sharks, which are found a few miles from the coast. They use nets for the purpose and the tails and fins are cut off and dried in the sun, suspended from a framework of poles. The dried fins and tails are exported to Malaysia and Singapore where they are used in the manufacture of medicines.

Prawn fishing is unknown on the Trucial coast though it is organized on large-scale commercial lines in Kuwait, Bahrain, and Qatar. The prawn fishing grounds do not extend on the southern shores of the Gulf beyond Qatar, as the sea-bed along the Trucial Coast is unsuited to prawns.

Across the peninsula in the Gulf of Oman, fish are even more abundant than they are in the Arabian Gulf. Natural fish resources off the Batinah Coast are among the largest in the world, and the Indian Ocean has been described as the last unfished ocean. It follows that Fujairah and the dependencies of Sharjah on the Batinah Coast are well placed for the development of a profitable fishing industry, though the waters are not well suited to trawling because the sea-bed is uneven and rocky. Furthermore, the continental shelf is narrow, and deep water is soon reached from the shore. Pelagic fish, however, are particularly abundant, especially tuna, Spanish mackerel, bonito, jacks, sailfish, merlin, sardines, and anchovy. The Trucial States Development Office was very active in pursuing the possibilities of developing fishing in the Gulf of Oman along modern lines. A fisheries station and a small slipway for the repair of fishing boats have been erected at Khor Fakkan. Dibba, situated north of Fujairah, is also thought to have possibilities of becoming an important fishing centre. In Kalba, small fish are dried in large quantities for sale as fertilizer. This has suggested the feasibility of developing a modern fish-meal industry, and preliminary investigations into this possibility are now being carried out.

During the past few years increasing attention has been given to the improvement of the fisheries on both sides of the peninsula. A Fisheries Adviser has been appointed and a fisheries research vessel has been commissioned and is stationed at Khor Fakkan. The Food and Agriculture Organization of the United Nations is undertaking a survey of the fisheries potential in the area, covering both the Arabian Gulf and parts of the Indian Ocean.

The local fishermen of the area are hard working and highly skilled in traditional techniques of fishing, but their skills are now somewhat outdated and the systems of fish processing and marketing can only be described as primitive. In the past the poverty of the area prevented modernization, but now that resources are available, there is every reason to expect considerable development. Development is possible on a worthwhile scale only if the industry is completely modernized, as there is little money to be gained from the old methods or from the sale of dried fish. The freezing and processing of fish would provide the basis for a more rewarding industry, but this requires the complete reorganization of the industry and the provision of ice factories, cold storage, warehouses, and improved market-places.

Reference to one or two sidelines in the fisheries industry may be of interest, though not in themselves of very great economic significance. In April 1968 it was announced that a consignment of fourteen turtles weighing about half a ton were being sent to Britain, the first consignment of its kind to be dispatched from the Trucial States. The natural history of the green turtle is unique, and indeed so fascinating that a digression on its breeding habits may not be regarded as out of place. The green turtles follow a definite and unalterable routine, seeking their "home beach" every second year of their adult life even though in the interim they may have travelled over 1,000 miles. On coming ashore the female searches for the place where she herself was born and if she does not find it, she will return the following night. Having found the place, she digs a round hole about two feet deep with her back flippers for her eggs, which she then covers with sand. She may lay up to five clutches, not leaving until all her clutches are laid. The eggs are the size of a table-tennis ball and very soft. There is a market for them in the Far East, but egg-collecting should be discouraged as it would mean the loss of too many young turtles. The eggs and the young turtles are very vulnerable, and it is estimated that the mortality rate from egg to young turtle is as high as 80 per cent.

There are possibilities for the development of trade in green turtles in Ras al Khaimah or Dubai, but it is essential that the breeding-grounds should be protected from dogs and other animals. The breeding-grounds need to be fenced in and small wire-mesh pounds constructed in the sea to protect the baby turtles from other fish. The market for green turtles is highly specialized and exacting, and would need to be built up with care.

A small but interesting sideline in the fisheries is the culture of ornamental tropical fish, which are highly prized by collectors and aquarium owners. A fish farm for this purpose has been started in Dubai on a small scale and might well be developed. In Hong Kong, for example, there are many ponds for the breeding of goldfish, and in Japan the breeding of brightly coloured carp is a sizeable industry and the hobby of collecting such fish is widespread in that country.

Chapter 8

Trade and Commerce

Economic prosperity in the United Arab Emirates depends on crude-oil production and trade, but whereas oil is a newcomer, trade and maritime enterprise have a long history which extends back 5,000 years or more. Throughout the ages, the Gulf has retained its importance as a great trade-route, though with varying fortunes. In the 19th century, the carrying trade was an important means of livelihood for the inhabitants of the coastal towns, despite the prevalence of piracy in the earlier decades. Between December and March, the sailing vessels made use of the north-east monsoon to take them down to Mombasa, Zanzibar, and Dar es Salaam, and then between April and September they returned with the south-west monsoon.

In the 20th century, competition from steam-ships and then the decay of the pearling industry brought hard times to the carrying trade and to the Gulf states in general. Trade with the outside world fell off as the coastal towns had little to offer in exchange and the inhabitants had to struggle on as best they could. Life was hard and frugal and their diet consisted of fish, dates, and imported rice; only occasionally would they have meat to eat. In the interior, the nomads carried on in their traditional ways, dependent on their animals. It has been estimated that during these lean years, from about 1930 until oil discoveries in Abu Dhabi transformed the situation, some 18,000 persons, nearly all adult males, left their homes in the Trucial States to seek work in the oil-producing countries of Bahrain, Kuwait, and Qatar, but lacking any special skills they had to undertake lower-paid manual jobs. They went as temporary migrants, remitting small sums of money home to their families, and few seem to have settled in their country of work.

The only exception in this land of poverty was Dubai, which through sheer enterprise was able to build up a commanding position as an entrepôt and trading city-state. Indeed, if any state in the Middle East has lifted itself up into economic prosperity by its own boot straps, it is Dubai. One-tenth the size of Switzerland and with a population of about 100,000, this small emirate without apparent natural resources must have seemed not so long ago as most unlikely ever to become much more than a minor port engaged in local trade and fishing. Opportunity, however, comes to him who seeks it, and against all the odds Dubai became a centre of the world gold trade and a flourishing entrepôt. The importance of Dubai as a trading centre can be gauged from the trading statistics which show that in 1974 Dubai imported goods to the value of £530 million, which works out at the remarkably high average of over £5,000 per head of the population. How, it may well be asked, has Dubai attained such a remarkable degree of economic prosperity without the help of oil exports until the end of 1969? The answer can only be that it rests on the inherent abilities of her rulers and her people and on their consistently liberal outlook, combined with a flair on the part of her merchants for entrepreneurship. The foundations of Dubai's prosperity in fact go back further than might be expected, for in the early years of the present century the then ruler encouraged Iranian and Indian merchants to settle in Dubai. A tradition of free enterprise was built up and has been fostered ever since. Liberal trade policies, moderate import duties, and minimal transit charges have reinforced the advantages of geographical location enjoyed by Dubai.

At the turn of the century the rise of Dubai as a trading centre was largely stimulated by the decline of Lingah after the Arab governorship there was abolished in 1902, and the Persians set up a customs' administration where previously there had been none. The effect was to drive much of Lingah's trade to the opposite side of the Gulf and in particular to Dubai. Thereafter Dubai's development was steady though not spectacular until 1957, when a meteoric rise took place. Import trade in 1958 was worth about £3 million, by 1960 it was over £6 million, in 1967 it was £42 million, and by 1969 it had soared to £81 million.

Dubai is now the major import centre and entrepôt of the eastern end of the Gulf and the main port of entry for imports into the northern states of the Federation as well as into the interior of Oman. Across the Gulf, it has a very active trade with southern Iran and with more distant parts, especially India and Pakistan. Dubai's prosperity was greatly increased by the trade in gold, which was bought on the open markets in London or Geneva and sold quite legally to syndicates of merchants who smuggled it into India and other countries. Some fifteen years ago, Kuwait and Bahrain were great smugglers, being very clever in their methods, but Dubai took over when oil development provided other outlets for Kuwaiti and Bahraini merchants. Beirut, too, up to some ten years ago, was a very important gold centre, but was by-passed when BOAC and MEA flights enabled gold to be carried direct to Dubai's improved airport. By 1966 Dubai was taking more gold (about £50 million worth) from the London market than any other country except France and Switzerland, itself an important buying market for Dubai merchants. Smuggling is no crime in Dubai, whatever the countries at the receiving end may feel about it, and smuggling is by no means confined to gold, other favourite articles for smuggling being watches. In recent years, gold smuggling has declined considerably.

The merchant community in Dubai is cosmopolitan. Indians, Iranians, and Pakistanis trade freely on equal terms with Arabs, and government regulations are kept to a minimum compatible with the needs for security and commercial good order. Commercial disputes are seldom brought to the courts but are settled by special tribunals appointed by the Ruler from among various panels of merchants selected for their knowledge of commercial matters and regardless of their nationality. There are no restrictions on the entry or repatriation of capital or the remittance of profits; nor are any such restrictions contemplated. Customs duties were levied at the moderate though unusual rate of 4·625 per cent on all dutiable goods, with the exception of rice, flour, wheat, and sugar, which were charged 2 per cent only. For goods in transit to Abu Dhabi, Oman, and Qatar, a transit rate of 2 per cent is levied. Alcoholic liquors, however, pay 25 per cent. There is a possibility that Dubai may be made a free-trade zone, but no decision has yet been taken on this matter. At present, gold bullion and other unworked precious metals are free of all duty, nor are there any restrictions or duty on their export. Books, printed matter, fresh fish, and agricultural produce from other members of the Federation are also allowed in free of duty. In 1973 customs duties were reduced to 3 per cent.

To facilitate trade and provide necessary services for exporters and importers, a Chamber of Commerce was opened in 1965. Membership is required for all firms engaged in trade or industry, and the objects of the chamber are to regulate and protect commercial and industrial interests in Dubai and to maintain close contacts with government departments in all matters affecting the interests of trade or industry. Arbitration facilities are available for the settlement of disputes between traders, and the chamber is empowered to issue Certificates of Origin for goods exported from Dubai.

Dubai Town and Deira, both part of the same single urban complex and separated only by the creek, present a very attractive appearance to the visitor. Offices, houses, warehouses, docks, and quays line both sides of the creek, giving an impression reminiscent of Venice, and this Italianate appearance is completed by the numerous wind-towers rising like campaniles from the older houses. The whole atmosphere is one of great animation and of bustling, purposeful activity, yet the town is pleasant enough to live in, and residents, native and expatriate alike, speak enthusiastically of its attractions. Numerous small ferry boats, known as *abra*, ply to and fro, threading their way among the many varied types of craft lying in the creek or busy loading or unloading at the quay-sides. These craft range from the fine-lined, fast-moving ships which are known locally as gold boats to sturdily-built *booms* engaged in the Gulf cargo trade. Less often seen now are the steel lighters which used to discharge cargoes collected from ocean-going ships too large to enter the creek. To compensate as it were for the loss of this traffic to the creek after the new port was built, its popularity with "country craft" (smaller boats engaged in local trade) has increased, and in addition there has grown up a large traffic in oil-company workboats and launches. Other fast launches are also to be seen which are engaged in effecting crew changes for oil-tankers sixty miles out.

Vessels of up to 800 tons only can anchor in the creek, and before Port Rashid was built larger ships had to stand outside about a mile from the creek and were served by the fleet of nine tugs and thirty steel lighters owned by Gray Mackenzie

Ltd. Now this double handling is avoided, and ships berth alongside the quays. This port owed its inception to the Ruler, Shaikh Rashid bin Sa'id al Maktum, who was determined that Dubai should not only retain its position as a great entrepôt but increase its importance. Shaikh Rashid, who succeeded in 1958, has been exceptionally energetic and broad-minded in promoting the development of his state, and combines progressive attitudes and business acumen with the traditional accessibility of the Arab Shaikh to all who need his counsel or help. Work commenced on the building of the port early in 1968 and was estimated to cost £25 million. The port now completed has fifteen alongside berths for ships drawing up to thirty feet, but it is intended to increase the number of berths still further. The work of construction proceeded rapidly, and the first two berths were handed over for operation on 19 November 1970, well in advance of schedule. By the end of 1971 there were eight berths in full operation, each with adjacent warehousing of 80,000 square feet and ample open storage available. Operation of the port, including marine services, landing facilities, cargo handling, storage, and delivery has been entrusted to Dubai Port Services, a company formed by Gray Mackenzie Ltd and incorporated in Dubai. This company took over on 1 January 1971, and the port itself was officially opened in October 1972, a full thirteen months ahead of schedule.

The value of imports into Dubai over the past twelve years has shown a remarkable increase from 109 million Dirhams in 1962 to 4,817 million in 1974. There was an especially big jump in 1968, when imports increased almost 60 per cent over those of the previous year. In 1970 and 1971, though the upward trend continued, the increases were much smaller than in the immediately preceding years. This was no doubt largely due to a slackening of activity which took place in Abu Dhabi during those years. Imports into Abu Dhabi from Dubai fell in 1970 to somewhat less than half what they had been in 1969. In 1972 Dubai's imports jumped by forty per cent over the previous year.

The leading countries of provenance in order over recent years have been Japan, the UK, Switzerland, the USA, India, West Germany, Pakistan, China, Hong Kong, Saudi Arabia, Holland, and Italy, with some small changes from year to year in their relative position. From 1966 Japan had been leading the UK but in 1971 the UK took first place. Switzerland had first place in 1966 and 1967 when the market was flooded with Swiss watches. (See Tables 12 and 13.) In 1972 the UK dropped to third place owing to large imports of oilfield equipment from the USA and of textiles from Japan.

There is a great deal of specialization among the supplying countries, as Dubai merchants are active in seeking out the best and cheapest sources of supply. A pipe smoker, for example, will find that in all probability his pipe will have come from Denmark, his tobacco from Holland, and his lighter from Austria. His lighter flints, however, will most likely have come from West Germany and his lighter fuel from the UK. He will find that nearly two thirds of the cigarettes smoked by his friends come from the UK and nearly a third from the USA. If they roll their own, the cigarette paper is likely to be French. Cigars are mainly Swiss, but the matches to light them will probably be Czechoslovakian.

Dubai merchants tend to tap all possible sources of supply, provided price and quality are favourable. Thus, in a recent year, cosmetics came from twenty-two different countries, ready-made garments from thirty-four, furniture from twenty-nine, and paint from twenty countries.

The variety of goods imported is astonishingly large and in the official analysis of imported commodities well over 500 varieties are distinguished, though some of them, such as tools, electrical appliances, or chemicals, are large groups in themselves.

Unfortunately it is not possible to trace how these imports are redistributed among the countries of the Gulf, as complete statistics relating to re-exports are not available since there is no legal requirement on exporters to provide manifests (lists of cargo) except for livestock. Consequently many re-exports go unrecorded.

TRADE AND COMMERCE IN ABU DHABI

During the boom years of 1968 and 1969, Abu Dhabi Town used to look like one gigantic building-site. In those years, construction provided employment for 40 per cent of the economically active population, and constructional materials accounted for 82 per cent in value of the total import bill.

Only 13 per cent of the working population in Abu Dhabi was concerned with trade, commerce, and transport, compared with 60 per cent in neighbouring Dubai.

This intense activity in construction dated back only to 1966, when Shaikh Zaid loosened the purse strings which had been so tightly held by his predecessor, Shaikh Shakbut.

Oil was discovered in Abu Dhabi in 1958. Before that year Abu Dhabi was an economic backwater with few trading or other contacts with the outer world, and her inhabitants had to eke out a frugal existence as fishermen or desert pastoralists. With the pearling industry in decay from 1930 onwards, their position was not to be envied. In the more distant past, however, the oasis of Al Ain, then known as Towwam, had constituted an important junction of the overland trade routes of south-east Arabia, but in the 20th century the flow of trade had ceased and the camel caravans had become an anachronism.

In 1967, the surge forward in construction brought with it a vast increase in the importation of materials of all kinds, which continued until 1969, when imports reached the astonishingly high level of DH 11,000 (£1,030) per head. In 1964, the corresponding value of imports is estimated to have been only DH 1,000 per head. There are as yet few industries of any importance in Abu Dhabi apart from oil, and consequently all constructional material including even stone for constructing the harbour have to be imported, as have also consumer durables, textiles, and most foodstuffs.

In 1970 and 1971 economic activity declined into a minor recession, and the proportion of the working population engaged in construction fell to about 19 per cent. Imports began to fall away in the last quarter of 1969, and there was a heavy fall in 1970, when imports were only 59 per cent of those in the previous year. In

1971 there was a partial recovery to about 80 per cent of the best year. Signs of a revival became apparent in the second half of 1971, and in 1972 construction shot ahead again and imports rose rapidly. Imports form a good barometer of what is happening in Abu Dhabi, and the figures can act as an indicator of what may happen on the economic front in the near future.

Comprehensive import figures, however, are available only from 1969, after the reorganization of the Customs Department. The statistics for the years before 1969 are incomplete, as they apply only to duty-paid imports and to that extent are misleading, especially as all imports by the oil companies for their own use and all materials imported by contractors working on government account are duty-free, as are certain foodstuffs.

Apart from construction goods, the largest imports consist of foodstuffs, household appliances, air conditioners, textiles, and cigarettes, in that order. Other items of importance are cosmetics, watches, and photographic goods.

The United Kingdom is the leading importer and has held this position for many years, providing about a third of all imports. The USA follows at some distance but considerably ahead of any of the other countries. Lagging considerably behind but next in order come Dubai and West Germany, except that in 1971 West Germany lost her place to Japan.

In Dubai, Japan and the UK tend to run neck and neck, with Japan usually a little ahead, though in 1971 the UK had the edge on Japan. The explanation of the different import structures lies in the differences in demand. Dubai is more consumer-oriented, whereas Abu Dhabi is at a stage where construction is the main source of activity, and Abu Dhabi is not engaged in re-export on the scale of Dubai. Abu Dhabi has no exports apart from oil, but there is a small amount of re-exporting. In 1971, the first year for which figures became available, re-exports totalled BD 4 million, that is, 9 per cent of the total exports. About half these re-exports went to Saudi Arabia, and consisted of oilfield equipment.

Imports arrive in Abu Dhabi by ocean-going ships, by local craft (*dhows*), by air, and by road. Naturally the great bulk of imports come by ocean vessels, and in 1974 the tonnage coming in this way was about 582,000. Local craft bring their cargoes from Bahrain, Qatar, Dubai, Kuwait, Saudi Arabia, Iran, and Oman. In 1971, the total tonnage arriving in these craft amounted to about 100,000 tons. Over 1,000 lorries a month come to Abu Dhabi, principally from Dubai but in increasing numbers from Ras al Khaimah, Sharjah, Ajman, and to a lesser extent Um al Quaiwain. Qatar, Kuwait, Fujairah, and Oman also send lorries direct to Abu Dhabi. In 1971 this lorry traffic carried some 44,000 tons, and it can be expected that road traffic will increase considerably in future years as roads are constructed linking Abu Dhabi with Dubai on the one side, and with Qatar and Kuwait on the other side. Air transport is of considerable importance for the carriage of perishables, mail, and urgent consignments. This traffic runs at over 7,000 tons inward and about 4,000 tons outward a year.

The import trade of Abu Dhabi in constructional materials will inevitably fall off when the initial development phase is completed, though this must be yet some years ahead, but it may be expected that trade in consumer goods will increase greatly as wealth spreads among the population as a whole and as the demand grows for raw materials for the new industries which it is hoped to establish.

Customs duties on goods imported into Abu Dhabi are low. Those coming direct from their country of origin used to pay $2\frac{1}{2}$ per cent while those imported from countries other than their country of origin paid 5 per cent. Alcoholic liquors paid 25 per cent, but certain foodstuffs were exempt, and, as stated earlier, so were imports of the oil companies and of contractors working on government account. There are now no customs duties on goods imported from the other emirates in the Federation. From 1 January 1975, customs duties were reduced to one per cent, and many commodities became dutyfree, including all kinds of foodstuffs, building construction materials, machinery, plant and equipment, medicines and agricultural requirements. The aim of the exemptions was to help to reduce the cost of living and constructional costs.

RAS AL KHAIMAH

In the past, Ras al Khaimah was an important trading centre, but that was many years ago and the emirate lost out in the changing economic climate of the early years of this century. Ras al Khaimah has no natural deep-water harbour, and even its creek was allowed to silt up. Nor until very recently were there any made roads, only tracks connecting it with the other states.

Now Ras al Khaimah is benefiting from the wind of change, and prospects are much brighter than they have been for a long time. The construction of new highways along the coast to Dubai, and of roads to Digdagga and elsewhere within the shaikhdoms, have transformed the situation and greatly encouraged the export of fresh fruit and vegetables to the other Gulf states, and in particular to Dubai and Sharjah. Dried fish is exported to India and Pakistan and there is an unusual export in the form of shark fins and tails to Far Eastern markets.

Though large ocean-going vessels still have to anchor in the roadstead and lighters have to be employed to land their cargoes, harbour facilities have been greatly improved. Two such improved harbours are now in operation, one the old harbour of Ras al Khaimah Town and the other at Khor Khowair, which lies half way between Rams and Sha'am. The Town harbour was improved and modernized in 1965 by means of a grant from the Trucial States Development Fund, and later in 1968 with the assistance of an American oil company, prospecting in an offshore concession, which built a 100-metre jetty and a breakwater. Plans are being discussed to dredge the inlet to a depth sufficient to accommodate vessels of twenty-five feet draught. The harbour at Khor Khowair was constructed for the special purpose of accommodating barges engaged in transporting stone from the local quarries to Abu Dhabi, where it was needed in the building of a new port there. Khor Khowair is equipped with modern loading and off-loading equipment, and will provide facilities for the export of cement to be produced by the Ras al Khaimah Cement Company, which is erecting its main plant near Khor Khowair and drawing its raw material from the quarries.

Britain and Japan are the main suppliers of consumer goods to the emirate, and

India and Iran supply large quantities of foodstuffs. More recently, imports of motor vehicles, electrical equipment, and machinery have been increasing, whereas only a few years ago imports were confined almost exclusively to foodstuffs and other consumer goods. Direct shipments into Ras al Khaimah at present amount in value to about DH 2 million while indirect shipments through Dubai amount to about DH 10 million a year.

Customs duties on imports into Ras al Khaimah are at the rate of 4 per cent *ad valorem* when arriving by road or in small native craft, but if they come in cargo ships the rate is reduced to 1 per cent. This is to encourage direct import. All foodstuffs and basic raw materials for development are allowed in duty-free. In other directions, too, encouragement is being given to development and to new enterprises. Small trading companies are licensed without much formality, and foreigners desiring to trade in the emirate are granted permits on showing a contract for a lease of premises covering a period of at least one year and presenting a personal or bank guarantee valid over the same period.

To protect the interests of traders, a Chamber of Commerce was established in 1967. It supervises the wholesale and retail trades and is active in promoting contacts between members and business firms abroad. It acts as an arbitrator in business disputes and acts as a link between the government and business.

An indicator of increasing economic activity in Ras al Khaimah is the growth in the number of banks operating in the emirate. A few years ago there was only the British Bank of the Middle East, but at the time of writing there are no fewer than six well-known banking houses operating in Ras al Khaimah.

THE OTHER EMIRATES

Among the other four states of the Federation, Sharjah is the most active in trade, but it is so close to Dubai that it is difficult to disentangle its activities in this field. Sharjah has its own airport and a harbour which had silted up but has now been dredged and improved to take small ocean-going vessels. Two ships can be accommodated at a time and a warehouse and a small boat harbour have been added. Customs duties are very moderate, being only $2\frac{1}{2}$ per cent *ad valorem*. Sharjah has an unusual export in the form of red oxide, which is mined in the Island of Abu Musa. A concession for exploiting this material is held by The Golden Valley Colours Ltd, a British company with a head office at Wick, near Bristol. The company also has concessions for mining in some nine or ten other islands including Sir bu Na'ir, where mining was once carried on but has been abandoned as the ore was found to be of an inferior quality. It appears that production has also been suspended in Abu Musa owing to the partial exhaustion of the more easily worked areas. The annual output of red oxide was about 16,000 tons a year and a small income accrued to the Ruler of Sharjah in the form of royalties on these exports. The red oxide ore is known in the trade as "Gulf Red" and is used as a colorant in the manufacture of paint and of cosmetics such as lipstick.

Sharjah's dependencies on the Batinah Coast—Kalba, Khor Fakkan, and Dibba—have good fertile land where citrus and other fruits and vegetables are cultivated, but there is little export except for small quantities of dried lemons, which go to other Gulf states and to Latin America. There are, however, considerable possibilities for the establishment of a valuable fishing industry using modern techniques, but at present the trade is confined to dried fish and fish manure. Development of these dependencies and of Fujairah, lying also on the Batinah Coast, depends on the improvement of transport facilities, on which a beginning is now being made.

The small states of Ajman and Um al Quaiwain have little trade, though here there are possibilities in the establishment of a modernized fishing industry. They have little if any direct trade, and imports come through Dubai, as do those of Fujairah. Fujairah has a small export of tobacco and dried lemons, the former being marketed in the region and the latter going mainly to Latin America.

Chapter 9

Industry and Industrial Development

Before proceeding to describe industrial development in the UAE, it would seem desirable to say something about industrial development in the Gulf states as a whole, because the emirates of Abu Dhabi and Dubai are likely to follow a pattern of development similar to that of the older oil-producing states of Kuwait, Bahrain, and Qatar. In these Gulf states, manufacturing industries are divided into two groups. One consists of large-scale, highly capitalized industries employing the most modern technology, export-oriented and based on oil or natural gas. The other group is composed of small, traditional and labour-intensive handicrafts working for a local market. In between there is a small though growing intermediate group, based like the first group on imported technology and machinery, but less highly capitalized and of more moderate size. For the most part, these industries serve local markets and are engaged in servicing, repair, and maintenance, or manufacture such articles as soft drinks or cement blocks, which if imported would involve high transport costs in relation to their value.

The group of large industries includes the oil refineries of Bahrain and Kuwait, the petro-chemical and fertilizer plants of Kuwait and Qatar, the aluminium smelter of Bahrain, and the prawn fisheries of Kuwait, Bahrain, and Qatar. All these plants or enterprises are export-slanted, their management is expatriate, and they are backed by foreign capital. For countries such as Kuwait, which has great financial resources derived from the export of oil but which has a relatively small indigenous population, capital-intensive industries are especially attractive.

The small traditional handicrafts are at the other extreme from the technologically-based industries. They work only for the local market and generally are very small, requiring little capital. Some are one-man businesses, but more usually the master-craftsman is assisted by members of his family or by two or three journey-men or apprentices. In the original sense of the word, these craftsmen are truly "manufacturers", as they work with their hands, using simple, traditional tools without the assistance of power-driven machines. The number and variety of these crafts still surviving in the Gulf are considerable. In all the larger and in many of the smaller towns, there are usually to be found bakers and sweet-makers, goldsmiths, silversmiths, and metal workers, tailors and sandal-makers, quilt-makers and sign-writers, carpenters and joiners, tent manufacturers and the makers of wire fish-traps. Formerly, potters, weavers, and wood-carvers were numerous, but these handicrafts have now practically disappeared, though boat-builders still struggle on with some success. In the past, fishing and shipping depended entirely on local craftsmen, who not only built the boats but also made the sails, ropes, and other gear.

The craftsmen of today are as highly skilled in their traditional trades as those of the past. They use their primitive tools with great expertise, as for example the woodturners who operate their simple lathes or drills using both their hands and their feet. Gradually, however, the old crafts are being driven out by the competition of imported machine-made goods, and many more of them will inevitably dis-appear before long, as the older skilled workers are not being replaced by younger men. Some of the small workshops, however, are meeting the challenge by mechanizing their operations and are able to stand up to the new competition by taking advantage of nearness to their markets, or by specializing on repair work, or by attention to the needs of individual customers, as in the tailoring trades.

Transition to modern methods of manufacture is most clearly to be seen in the intermediate-group industries. Notable among them is the manufacture of soft drinks, as this is eminently well-suited to the Gulf by reason of climate and of the high cost of imports. A similar industry is the bottling of gas for domestic use. An industry which has grown enormously in recent years is motor repair and main-tenance. The trend as exemplified in Kuwait is towards specialization; some firms concentrate on body repairs or panel-beating and others on radiators, springs, car seats, or electrical equipment.

The establishment of intermediate industries, especially those of somewhat larger size such as cement block manufacture, asphalt plants, ship repairing, paint manufacture, plastics, or flour milling, is bringing much needed diversification to the economy of the countries and gradually more and more fields of activity are being opened up. Two important factors helping to increase the numbers of these establishments are the supply of electrical energy and road improvements. Electri-city provides a convenient and cheap form of power, while road improvements, by bringing the more remote parts of the country into easy contact with the towns, increase the size of the potential market.

In the UAE, the lead in industrial development is understandably being taken by Abu Dhabi, because of its rapid rise as an oil-exporting state. Its crude-oil industry is highly capitalized, highly automated, and still rapidly expanding. Oil production in Abu Dhabi began only in 1962, nearly thirty years later than in Bahrain, twenty years later than in Qatar, and ten years later than in Kuwait. Abu Dhabi, however, proved to be a very vigorous infant, and within five years crude oil was being produced at an annual rate of about 18 million long tons. By the end of the following five years, production was boosted to an annual rate of some 44 million long tons. The government's income from oil-taxation and royalties rose at a much faster rate owing to 'the negotiation of more favourable terms. These oil revenues provided the key to economic progress in the emirate, but at first progress was relatively slow owing to the cautious attitude of the Ruler, Shaikh Shakbut; but when he was succeeded by his brother, Shaikh Zaid, the position changed and development shot ahead. A Five-Year Plan was drawn up envisaging an expenditure of BD 297 million (£260 million sterling) over the five years from 1968 to 1972.

Development of the oilfields naturally preceded other developments, as oil export provided the spring which drives the economy. The oil companies exemplify private enterprise in a highly sophisticated form, but among the inhabitants of Abu Dhabi there was no tradition of private enterprise of a type which would lead to the organization and establishment of modern factories, workshops, or service industries. Moreover, at this stage a prime necessity was the building-up of an infra-structure of roads, communications, and public utilities. Hence it was largely left to the government to take the initiative. The emphasis was on construction, and when private enterprise began to follow the government lead in development it concentrated on the construction of shops, offices, and apartment blocks, to the neglect of industry.

The government in general did not employ direct labour in its construction activities, but sought the advice of international consultants and put out the actual work of construction to contractors under a system of competitive bidding. The years 1968 and 1969 were peak years in constructional activity. In those years some 12,000 persons were engaged on construction out of a total work force of some 29,000, that is, 40 per cent of the total. Private enterprise during these two years was also active in construction and many new office and apartment blocks were built. In 1969, constructional materials accounted for 82 per cent of total imports by tonnage.

In 1970 constructional activity fell off, and the economy suffered a set-back owing to previous over-spending and did not revive appreciably until about the middle of 1971. By that time, however, many large constructional projects were completed or near completion, including the corniche, the main urban road system, the airport, a new electricity generating station, and a water-distillation plant.

In 1972, the economy had picked up and construction again became almost feverish, with many new buildings being erected and others which had been left partly finished being given added storeys or extensions. The demand for offices and apartments seemed insatiable, and was stimulated by the fact that Abu Dhabi Town had become the capital of the Federation, with new ministries, embassies, and legations all seeking accommodation.

With the infra-structure largely completed, the stage is now set for the establishment of new industries, which the government is seeking to introduce with the object of diversifying the economy. Projects now at the planning stage or under construction include a refinery, a cement plant, a flour mill, a lime-sand brick factory, an LNG plant, bottled-gas plant and a steel mill. Other projects under consideration are the manufacture of sulphur, sulphuric acid, caustic soda, plastics and spiral-welded pipes. The establishment of petro-chemical industries is being considered.

Private enterprise has also begun to enter the manufacturing field and a number of small industries have already been established, including soft drinks manufacture, printing presses, cement block making, commercial poultry farming, ice-making, and the fabrication of windows, doors, and shop-fittings. Suggested new industries for the private sector include the manufacture of vehicle tyres, car batteries, soap, paper goods and matches. The service industries, which in 1971 employed 17 per cent of the total work force, are likely to increase greatly with general economic expansion. Large hotels of international standard, cinemas, supermarkets, and outside catering services are well established, and there are many petrol and service stations, laundries, garages, and tailoring establishments. No census of industry or trade has yet been undertaken in the Federation, but a survey of retail shops, service industries, and workshops which was completed for Abu Dhabi State in the autumn of 1972 gave a total of 2,340 such establishments, employing 8,302 persons. In the retail trade, grocers' shops followed by those selling clothing were the most numerous; among the service industries, coffee shops and restaurants followed by the tailors predominated; and among the workshops, motor repair and maintenance greatly outnumbered all the others.

In the other six emirates, manufacturing industry is little developed, accounting for barely 4 per cent of the total labour force. Dubai, though economically very active, is mainly engaged in commerce and foreign trade. It now has its own oilfield, off shore, which is highly automated and has a unique system of submerged storage tanks. In 1973 its production amounted to 11 million long tons, but it is increasing. There are many retail shops in Dubai, and a number of flourishing service industries including printing presses, hotels, high-class restaurants, cinemas, and even a night-club or two. There are among established industries an asbestos pipe factory, a cement plant and two paint factories, and it may reasonably be expected that many other industrial enterprises will emerge as oil revenues mount and the economy takes on a new form, combining its commercial expertise with developments in manufacture. The most ambitious project at present under construction is the building of a huge dry-dock capable of handling the largest oil-tankers afloat.

In Ras al Khaimah a cement plant with a capacity of 250,000 tons a year has been constructed at an estimated cost of DH 60 million with financial assistance from Abu Dhabi. The proximity of suitable supplies of stone and of adequate harbour facilities makes this a very suitable industry for Ras al Khaimah. Supplies of marble also exist and may enable a marble quarrying, cutting and polishing industry to be established. In several of the emirates there are possibilities for setting up modern fish-processing factories, as for example in Ajman and Um al Quaiwain, and especially on the Batinah Coast at Khor Fakkan or Kalba.

Small crafts of the *suq* (bazaar) type are to be found in all the towns though not on the same scale as in Dubai. These cover a wide variety of trades and occupations, such as carpenters' shops, bakeries, cafés, silversmiths, goldsmiths, metal working, barbers, laundries, or tailoring. The number engaged in these crafts and services, however, is not very large and their scale of operation is very small. A rough estimate of the number of such establishments in the seven emirates would not be more than about 4,000.

To round off this survey of industries and industrial development, something needs to be said of the public-utility industries such as water supplies and electricity production. Experience in all countries shows that the demand for these services tends to grow as economic expansion outpaces the growth of population, and this generalization applies in no uncertain fashion to the UAE.

In Abu Dhabi Town before 1964, the main water supply came from somewhat salty wells known as *Kharijah*, but sweet water had to be imported at a cost, it is related, of about six dinars a barrel and double that during the hot summer months. In 1964 a nine-inch pipe-line was constructed to connect the town with wells in the Sa'ad district of Al Ain. A regular supply of good water was thus secured, but the deliveries proved inadequate even though fifteen wells had been tapped. In 1967, a second and larger pipe-line, this time eighteen inches in diameter was constructed, bringing the total water supply up to 1·7 million gallons a day. Demand, however, still continued to rise and the town was faced with a serious water shortage, so that it became necessary to install a sea-water distillation plant. This plant, now in commission, is integrated with a new electricity generating station and is capable of producing 6 million gallons of water a day.

Dubai, like Abu Dhabi, used to have to depend on shallow wells for a supply of water, but this brackish supply was replaced in 1961 by water extracted from a sand bed some distance from the town. Production initially was 400,000 gallons a day but is now about 4 million gallons a day, and a piped distribution system is complete in the town and is being extended to outlying areas.

Ras al Khaimah Town is supplied with water from wells situated at Al Breirat, about fifteen kilometres away, which supply not only the Town but also Rams and Jezirat. A piped water supply has been made available to the villages along the coast over a distance of twenty-five kilometres. Other villages inland are supplied with water from artesian or other wells.

The Trucial States Development Council gave special attention to the boring of wells throughout the northern states, and now most sizeable villages have their water supply. Sharjah obtained a fresh water supply in 1965, when a pipe-line was completed connecting wells at Bidaya, some twelve miles distant from the towns.

Supplies of electricity are now available in all the capital towns of the Federation and are gradually being extended to many of the smaller towns. In Abu Dhabi Town, the demand for electrical energy appears to be almost insatiable and in the five years from 1969 to 1974 production increased four-fold with a still unsatisfied potential demand. The peak demand occurs during the summer months between mid-August and mid-September, when air-conditioning is now regarded not as a luxury but as an essential. The summer peak is five times the lowest trough, which occurs usually about mid-January. At first diesel engines only were used to drive the generators, but additional capacity has since been provided by gas and steam turbines supplied with fuel brought from the Muban field through a special gas pipe-line. A 33,000-volt network has been constructed linking the power station with eighteen distribution centres in Abu Dhabi Town. In Al Ain a similar network has been built linking the generating station with twelve distribution centres. Small generating units, independent of the main network, have been provided for some 15 rural areas, including for example Dalma Island, Beda Zayed, Wathbu, Beda Melawa or Al Yahar.

In Dubai, the Dubai Electricity Company was inaugurated in 1959 to meet the growing requirements of consumers, who up to then had to rely on privately-owned generators supplying a limited number of houses. The new station was completed in 1961 and had four generators of 360 kilowatts each. Since then, to meet constantly increasing demand, the capacity of the generating stations has been increased by stages to 45,000 kilowatts in 1970. As in Abu Dhabi, transmission is through a 33,000-volt network, stepped down in two stages to 220 volts for local distribution.

In Ras al Khaimah, the first power house was built in 1965, but before that a few small generators provided all the electricity that was needed. Capacity has grown to 3,100 kilowatts but this is being increased to 9,000 kilowatts through the erection of a new power house. This will supply power to the new cement factory as well as meeting all the requirements of Ras al Khaimah Town. It will also supply power to Rams and the island of Za'ab, now served by two 150 kilowatt generators. The electricity services of Ras al Khaimah are administered by a special government board which has a measure of independent authority for technical and staff matters.

In the smaller capitals and towns, the Development Council was active in providing and at first in running generating stations and distribution systems, including those in Ajman, Um al Quaiwain, Dibba, and Falaj al Mu'alla. In early 1971 most of these were handed over to their respective governments.

As the larger towns became still larger the disposal of sewage became an urgent problem, and both in Dubai and Abu Dhabi large modern sewage disposal systems have been undertaken. In Abu Dhabi the sewage scheme was first proposed in 1967, when it was decided that the normal drainage system working by gravity would be unsuitable because of the topography of the town and the high water-table. The town has been divided into eighteen areas for sewage disposal, and sewage from each of these is delivered in pipes to area pumping-stations, which in turn deliver the sewage to a central pumping-unit for onward transmission to the treatment works. The purified sewage water will be available for agriculture and is expected to reach a rate of about 1 million gallons daily. The system is highly automated, and any failure in any part of the system is notified to the central office at the main pumping-station by an automatic signalling device.

In Dubai, a modern sewage disposal system has been built, which provides a network of sewers discharging by gravity to subsidiary pumping-stations. These are connected to two main pumping-stations from which the sewage is passed to a treatment works. The effluent consisting of the purified water will be used for irrigation. Work started on the scheme at the end of 1968 and by 1971 was already partially completed.

It is obvious to both residents and visitors that great progress has been made in developing the economies of the seven emirates which compose the UAE, but it is difficult to find any measures which can be used to quantify that progress. Perhaps the best single measure would be that of national income expressed on a per caput basis, and the author has often been asked to provide such a figure. It is, however, extremely difficult and hazardous to give an answer, as the basic statistics for making the calculation do not exist and are now only gradually being collected and analysed. In consequence it is possible at present to give only very tentative estimates based on the best available material. The necessarily imperfect calculations made by the author indicate that in 1967 the national income for the seven states taken together was about 1,140 million Dirhams (say $300 million). This would amount to 6,330 Dirhams ($1,600) per caput. Five years later, in 1971, on a similar basis of calculation, the national income per caput amounted to about 10,500 Dirhams ($2,600). Now in 1975 it is something between 60 thousand and 76 thousand Dirhams a head ($15,000 to $19,000), or about $7 billion in total. The per caput average is of course very much of a statistical abstraction as the figures do not mean (national income figures never do) that on average each person has the equivalent in his pocket. National income takes account of capital formation and, for example, the money equivalent of state activities which provide education, health services, social welfare, and defence. National income, in short, takes account of much more than the spendable money of the individual. To avoid misconception, it needs perhaps to be emphasized that the figures given above apply to the Federation as a whole. The per caput national income for Abu Dhabi, with its vast oil exports, is much greater, perhaps something of the order of DH 25,000 per caput in 1971. By 1973 it had increased still further to about DH 30,000 per caput and to DH 80,000 (say $20,000) per caput in 1974.

Chapter 10

Money, Banking, and Finance

Throughout the Gulf area in the past, Maria Theresa dollars, Turkish coins, and Indian rupees served as currency; there were no local currencies issued in any of the shaikhdoms. Gradually, as a result of close commercial and political ties with India, the rupee became accepted as the main currency except inland, where Maria Theresa dollars continued to circulate. Acceptance of the rupee as a common currency greatly facilitated trade among the various shaikhdoms, India, and Muscat Oman. The system of free exchange and easy convertibility, however, eventually came to work rather too well from the point of view of the Indian government, as it also encouraged the smuggling of gold into India, entailing a substantial drain on that country's limited foreign exchange reserves. In 1957 and 1958, this drain assumed serious proportions, and the Indian government decided to restrict the convertibility of those rupee notes which circulated in the Gulf by issuing a new "Gulf rupee", which was not legal tender in India though having the same equivalent of 13·33 rupees to the pound sterling. The Gulf rupees were issued by the Reserve Bank of the Government of India, but were dyed red to distinguish them from their Indian counterparts issued by the same institution.

As a result of this restriction, which was very unpopular in the Gulf, there was a gradual move out of the rupee. The first Gulf state to abandon the rupee was Kuwait, which in 1961 established a currency of her own. The Kuwaiti dinar was sub-divided into 1,000 fils and was linked to sterling, with the dinar exactly equivalent to the pound. Bahrain followed in 1965, also with a dinar linked to sterling, but the Bahrain dinar was given a par value of 15 shillings, which was then the equivalent of ten rupees.

Transition to the new currencies was effected smoothly, and for a time Gulf rupees were allowed to circulate side by side with the new dinars to give a breathing space for redemption. In both countries there appears to have been only a slight effect on their price levels, which rose by about 1 per cent owing to the rounding-up of certain prices to the nearest convenient number of fils, without a corresponding reduction in appropriate cases. There was, however, a tendency among shoppers to exaggerate the rise and there was a general feeling that undue advantages were taken of consumers.

For the purpose of issuing and redeeming the new currency Kuwait set up a Currency Board with Bank of England guidance. The board was required to hold against the currency which it issued 100 per cent reserve in the form of gold and securities in US dollars and sterling. The Bahrain Currency Board, constituted in December 1964, was very similar to that of Kuwait and was also launched with guidance from the Bank of England. Approximately 20 per cent of Bahrain's currency is covered by gold and the remainder by foreign government securities and Treasury Bills.

About the same time as the Bahrain dinar was introduced, the other states of the Gulf were becoming dissatisfied with the Gulf rupee and were considering the advisability of adopting new currencies. Soon, however, events outside their control practically decided the matter for them. The first event was the withdrawal early in 1966 by the Reserve Bank of India of what had been normal facilities for the conversion into sterling of coins repatriated from the Gulf states. This was done in a further attempt to hinder the gold smugglers. To help meet the new situation the Bahrain Currency Board and the commercial banks in Bahrain made available considerable amounts of Bahraini coins against payments in sterling. Then, in June 1966, the Indian government devalued the rupee by somewhat over 35 per cent, fixing a new rate of exchange of 21 rupees to the pound sterling, but left it uncertain whether the devaluation applied to the Gulf rupee as well. The banks in the Gulf suspended dealings in Gulf rupees on the day of devaluation pending clarification of the position, which was complicated by the large sums involved, estimated to be the equivalent of some £14 million sterling. Clarification came a few days later, and it was then made clear that the devaluation applied equally to the Gulf rupee, even though this had previously been regarded as external currency. This put all the states using the Gulf rupee in difficulties, so Qatar and the seven Trucial States decided to sever their connection with the rupee immediately. Abu Dhabi adopted the Bahrain dinar and the others temporarily went over to the Saudi Arabian riyal. The governments of Qatar and Dubai supported the Gulf rupees circulating in their areas by replacing them with riyals for a period of three months. In the meantime a new Currency Board was established, known as the Qatar-Dubai Currency Board, with responsibility for the issue and redemption of a new currency which was named the Qatar-Dubai riyal, or QDR for short. This new riyal was issued and made legal tender in September 1966, when the Saudi riyal was withdrawn from circulation in the new currency area. The QDR was given a parity of 13·33 riyals to the pound sterling and was divided into 100 dirhams. The QDR was, in effect, of equivalent denomination to the former un-devalued Gulf rupee. The headquarters of the Qatar-Dubai Currency Board was situated in Dubai, where the National Bank of Dubai acted as its official agent.

The QDR quickly became established as the accepted currency in all the Trucial States other than Abu Dhabi, but it was readily exchangeable into Bahrain dinars in all these states and was accepted by shops, taxi drivers, and traders without difficulty, apart from some hotels which took a small commission on payments made in dinars. In Abu Dhabi, riyals were freely accepted at the rate of one riyal to 100 fils or ten riyals to the dinar. The general acceptance of interchangeability between Bahrain dinars and Qatar-Dubai riyals was made easier by the fact that the Bahrain dinar was exactly equivalent to ten QDR.

Abu Dhabi, as previously stated, joined the Bahrain dinar currency area in June 1966, but all the initial capital required to set up the board had been provided by the Bahrain government. On the other hand, Abu Dhabi shared neither in the management nor in the profits of the board. These profits arose from interest received on the investments of the board's capital in foreign securities and Treasury Bills.

The functions of the currency boards were to issue local currency against payment of sterling in London and to redeem the local currency against sterling deposits in London and the payment of a small commission. The boards were responsible for ensuring that any currency they issued was fully backed by reserve funds consisting of gold, sterling, sterling securities, or foreign currencies convertible into gold or sterling. The boards managed the currency reserve funds but they did not provide any of the other services normally associated with a central bank other than the collection and compilation of commercial banking statistics.

There were far more Bahrain dinars circulating in Abu Dhabi than in Bahrain. In 1969, Abu Dhabi's share may have been as high as BD 12 million out of a total of some 20 million, but the amount cannot be stated with accuracy as, though currency issued by the board for use in Abu Dhabi was known as well as that withdrawn, the amount which filtered backwards or forwards through trade or other channels was unknown. A similar difficulty applied to the QDR, which circulated both in Qatar and in the United Arab Emirates.

When Britain devalued the pound sterling in November 1967, neither of the two currency boards followed suit, and they had therefore to add to their reserves in order to maintain the 100 per cent cover for their currencies in circulation. In the case of Bahrain this involved a sum of BD 815,000. Under the Basle Agreement of 1968, however, some protection against any future devaluation was provided for the currency boards. By this agreement, sterling area central banks and currency boards agreed to maintain a minimum sterling proportion in their reserves, and in return they were exempt from British exchange controls and received a guarantee that they would be reimbursed (in sterling) for their losses should the pound be devalued below $2·38.

When the pound sterling was floated on 23 June 1972, there was a period of uncertainty as to whether the Bahrain dinar and the QDR would float along with the pound. On 1 July following, this uncertainty was removed by official announcements that neither currency would be floated but would remain linked in the case of the dinar to 1·86621 grams of fine gold, and in that of the riyal to 0·18662 grams.

Before the pound was floated, there had been discussions about a common currency for all the emirates of the Federation, and on 20 May 1973 a new currency for all the emirates constituting the UAE was introduced. This is the Dirham (DH), which is divided into 100 Fils and superseded both the Bahrain Dinar and the Qatar Dubai Riyal. The rates of exchange adopted were 10 Dirhams to the Bahrain Dinar and one Dirham to the Qatar Dubai Riyal, but after November 1973 the Dirham was allowed to float according to market forces in relation to the Bahrain Dinar and all other currencies. The Dirham has a fixed parity of 0·18621 grammes fine gold (0·21 of the International Monetary Fund's S.D.R.), and it has proved to be a strong currency. The rate of exchange in mid-1974 was around DH 9·40 to 9·52 to the pound sterling, depending on the fluctuations in the value of the latter, and DH 3·93395 to the US dollar. A year later, in mid-1975, the rates had become more favourable to the Dirham, with the pound sterling worth barely nine Dirhams. The UAE is in the fortunate position of having ample supplies of foreign exchange and there has been no balance of payments problem.

The currency is issued and regulated by the UAE Currency Board with offices in both Abu Dhabi and Dubai. In 1973, the Board instituted a forward exchange market, the only one in the Gulf area, with the object of facilitating international operations. In the autumn of 1974, the British guarantee against a fall in the value of sterling below $2·38 was withdrawn.

BANKING IN THE UNITED ARAB EMIRATES

Not so many years ago there were only two banking houses represented in Trucial Oman, namely the Eastern Bank (now the Chartered Bank) and the British Bank of the Middle East (BBME). Today over forty banking firms are operating, many of them with offices in several of the emirates. Among them are to be found well-known banking names from Britain, the USA, Pakistan, Iran, Canada, India, France, Lebanon, Bangladesh and Jordan, while yet other banking institutions from Germany and France participate through connections with locally chartered banks. There are many main bank offices, apart from sub-branches, in an area which has a population of about 600,000. Many of the banks have a number of sub-branches, notably in Abu Dhabi and Dubai, so that the grand total of bank offices licensed by the Currency Board amounted to 278 in January 1975, when the Board called a halt to further expansion. In addition, four foreign banking houses have been permitted to open representative offices. Branches of two foreign merchant banks and two locally incorporated finance companies have already been established, giving a new dimension to the financial structure of the Federation. In addition there are a number of local money-changing establishments known as *sarafs* working in the *suqs*, which have high traditions of commercial integrity and have their own chain of correspondents throughout the region and beyond.

The nature of banking in the Gulf differs considerably from the typical work of a bank in Britain, Germany, or America. The Gulf banks are concerned to a greater degree than their counterparts with the import and export trades: opening of letters of credit, collecting payments from importers, and the like. They also handle a considerable volume of foreign exchange business at all their offices and sub-branches, whereas in England, for example, the banks tend to handle such work in a few branches specializing in that field. Current accounts are nothing like as widespread as in Britain. During recent years, however, there has been a marked growth in the number of small savings-bank accounts, and it would appear reasonable to expect that many of the small savers will eventually hold current accounts. The Gulf banks, unlike those of Germany, do not participate directly in the financing of industry or constructional activities, apart from overdraft facilities.

A recent trend has been the setting up of sub-branches by the established banks in Abu Dhabi and Dubai, indicating a desire by the banks to extend their services more widely throughout the community and possibly also to increase their competitive attractions. It also indicates the increasing prosperity of these two capital towns. Assets of the banks in Abu Dhabi were almost DH 900 million at 31 December 1969; though they fell off in 1970, representing a slackening of economic activities, they climbed back again in 1971, and rose to DH 1,410 million in December 1972.

Savings and liquid resources are still held by the local population very generally in cash outside the banking system, and many commercial transactions are carried out in cash, by-passing the banks. It is not unusual to see a merchant when making a payment bring out a huge wad of notes. This penchant for cash payments is not due to any attempt to conceal profits from tax authorities, for there is no income tax; rather it is due to the persistence of old habits and traditions. The preference for cash payments is shown statistically by the high proportion of currency notes of the largest denominations circulating in the two currency areas.

BANKING IN DUBAI

Expansion of banking facilities in Dubai is fairly recent, as before 1963 there was only one bank operating there. This was the British Bank of the Middle East, which with its sub-branch in Sharjah had a monopoly dating back to 1946. By 1970 there were eighteen banking houses represented in Dubai, among which three were British, two Pakistani, two Iranian, two American, one Jordanian, and three locally chartered. By January 1975 the number had risen to 31, having between them 92 branch offices serving the public. All provide a full range of banking services, though they are largely concerned with trading and foreign exchange. One of the banks, namely the Commercial Bank of Dubai, is a joint venture in which Commerzbank AG of West Germany, the Chase Manhattan Bank of New York, and the Commercial Bank of Kuwait, as well as local shareholders, are represented. Banking business in Dubai was largely nurtured on the gold trade, and Dubai's growth as an entrepôt over the past ten years owes a great deal to the wealth accumulated by the gold merchants. Gold smuggling from the Gulf to India goes back to the 1930s, but in those earlier days it was mainly in the hands of Kuwaitis, who adopted most ingenious methods to outwit the Indian authorities. With the rapid increase in their wealth from oil, with the growing difficulties placed in the way of smugglers, such as the banning of Kuwaitis from entry to India, except as tourists, and with the introduction of the Gulf rupee, which was not legal tender in India, the Kuwaiti merchants withdrew from the gold trade, and this gave an opportunity for Dubai merchants to take over, which they did some fifteen years ago. The Dubai mer-

chants found that large profits were still possible despite the greater risks of inter-
ception, because of the wide gap between the London price of gold ($35 per ounce)
and the selling price of $68 or more in India. No statistics are available regarding
the amount of gold that found its way to India and the Far East, but estimates have
been made which place it at about £90 million a year. Smuggling was highly
organized and was carried out by syndicates of merchants, thus spreading the risks.
It was not confined to gold but extended to many other commodities, such as
watches. Recently there have been indications that the gold trade is not so lucrative
as it was in the past, and possibly, like Kuwait, Dubai may relinquish the trade to
other centres as alternative outlets open up for its enterprising merchants.

The British Bank of the Middle East had a monopoly in Dubai under its concession until 1963, when the National Bank of Dubai was chartered by the Ruler.
This bank is locally owned and acted as agent for the Qatar-Dubai Currency Board,
issuing and redeeming currency. The third bank to open in Dubai was the First
National City Bank of New York, which obtained special permission from the US
Treasury to deal in gold. Thereafter the number of banks increased rapidly and now
includes several other locally chartered banks, including the Bank of Oman, which
is owned by a group of Dubai merchants, the Commercial Bank, and the Bank of
Dubai. The assets held by the banks in Dubai increased rapidly after 1965 and were
the equivalent of over £80 million at the end of 1969. Deposits at the same date
amounted to some £28 million and bank advances to somewhat over £29 million.
Lending in proportion to deposits is of a high order, and the demand for loans
tends to favour those banks which can draw on funds outside Dubai. At the end of
1972, assets had risen to nearly £200 million.

BANKING IN ABU DHABI

There are at the time of writing thirty-one banks operating in Abu Dhabi, the same
number as in Dubai but not identical in composition. Three of these are the
customary triumvirate of British banking houses in the region, namely the British
Bank of the Middle East, the Chartered Bank, and Grindlays Bank. Pakistan is
represented by the United Bank and the Habib Bank, Dubai by the National Bank
of Dubai and the Bank of Oman, Iran by the Bank Saderat Iran and the Distributors'
Co-operative Credit Bank-Iran, America by the First National City Bank, and
Jordan by the Arab Bank. Complementing this spread of international interest,
there is Abu Dhabi's own bank, known as the National Bank of Abu Dhabi. This
bank has a capital of 1 million Bahrain dinars, with 85 per cent of its shares held
locally, 5 per cent by the National Westminster Bank, and the remaining 10 per
cent by other banking interests. All the 31 banks have offices in Abu Dhabi Town
and many, notably the Bank of Credit and Commerce, the British Bank of the
Middle East, the National Bank of Abu Dhabi and the United Bank, have a number
of sub-branches in developing districts of the town or in Al Ain. In all, 82 offices
are open to the public.

BANKING IN SHARJAH

After Dubai and Abu Dhabi with their 31 banking houses each, Sharjah has the most developed banking system in the Federation, with 23 banks represented, though its population is probably not much more than 88,000 persons. The initial impetus to banking was given by the British connection, Sharjah having been at one time a staging point for the flying boats of Imperial Airways and until 1971 a British military base, as well as the headquarters of the Trucial Oman Scouts. The banking houses represented in Sharjah include the usual three British banks: BBME, the Chartered Bank, and Grindlays Bank; two Pakistani Banks: Habib and United; and two Iranian banks: Bank Saderat and Bank Melli. The other banks include the Bank of Sharjah, the Commercial Development Bank of Sharjah, the National Bank of Abu Dhabi, Commercial Bank of Dubai, First National City, First National Bank of Chicago, Bank of Credit and Commerce, and Lebanese, Egyptian, Dutch and Indian banks.

BANKING IN THE OTHER STATES

A few years ago the only bank in the four remaining states was a branch of the British Bank of the Middle East in Ras al Khaimah. Now all the states have at least ten banks, including Ajman and Um al Quaiwain. Ajman indeed has eleven banks, including the Ajman Arab Bank. Um al Quaiwain has twelve banks; Fujairah has nine, of which the National Bank of Abu Dhabi has three branches, while BBME and Habib Bank have two each, giving a total of thirteen branches.

THE GENERAL POSITION OF BANKING

Considering that there are fifty banks operating in the United Arab Emirates, apart from sub-branches, which increase every year, there can be very little profit to be earned by many of them. Obviously the aim has been to obtain a foothold in the hope that rapid economic development over the next five years or so will justify the initial losses. Some of the banks, notably those well-established in Abu Dhabi and Dubai, of course do very well, though competition is increasing.

Control of banking activities until recently was practically non-existent. Permission to operate had to be obtained from the Ruler by foreign banks, while new local banks required a charter from the Ruler, but, beyond the conditions laid down in the licence, concession, or charter, there was no further control. The currency boards were concerned only with the issue and redemption of coins and notes and with the provision of a few statistics. Nevertheless all the banks had worked on sound banking lines. The prestige and presence of world-famous foreign banks had a good influence, and there were no apparent signs of unwise extension of credit, non-liquidity, or overstrain. The new locally chartered banks have been influenced by the example of the older banks, and most of them have appointed experienced British or other foreign managers to run their institutions.

It became apparent, however, in 1973 that some regulation was essential to prevent the banking system getting out of hand through competitive pressures among the rapidly increasing number of banks already operating and the long queue waiting to be admitted. The newly formed Currency Board therefore took a number of steps to regulate banking operations, including the prescribing of a ceiling on the interest rates paid by the banks on local currency deposits. In January 1975 the Board laid down that no more foreign banks would be permitted to open offices in the Federation over a period of two years, and that existing banks would only be allowed to open new branches where additional services were considered necessary. The only qualified exception is that locally incorporated banks with a share capital of not less than 80 per cent contributed by local interests might be licensed at the discretion of the Board.

ABU DHABI INVESTMENT AUTHORITY

Early in 1976, the Abu Dhabi Investment Authority was formed to replace the former London-based Abu Dhabi Investment Board. The new authority will take over the government's foreign investment portfolios of around $2,000 million as well as becoming responsible for investing new funds allocated for foreign investment.

Chapter 11

Transport and Communications

Improvements in transport, so aptly described by Adam Smith 200 years ago as "the greatest of all improvements", have been the most important factor contributing to the opening up of the Arabian Peninsula and to the transformation of the economic, cultural, and social life of the region. Should wealth from oil be likened to a dynamo providing the energy for economic growth and expansion, then transport and communications may be said to be the distribution network through which that energy is spread over the economy. Improvements in transport and communications have opened up Trucial Oman, brought remote places into easy contact with the main centres, spread the benefits of educational, health, and social services to all parts, raised standards of living by giving opportunities of employment where before there were none, other than in primitive fishing or pastoral occupations, lowered the cost of necessaries, subdued the desert, and indicated new horizons to the ordinary man.

In each state of the United Arab Emirates there is a certain degree of economic specialization possible, but without adequate transport facilities such potential development would lie dormant. Abu Dhabi is rich in oil, Dubai is active and progressive in trade and commerce, Ras al Khaimah can provide an agricultural base, Ajman and Um al Quaiwain can develop fishing industries, Sharjah could be a centre for service industries, and her dependencies on the Batinah Coast along with Fujairah might well develop into exporters of agricultural products and of processed and frozen fish. Development of the United Arab Emirates depends on some such degree of co-operation in diversification, and transport and communications are the essential link.

ROAD TRANSPORT

An extensive network of roads is now gradually being built up which eventually will link all the larger towns in the emirates and will serve local needs. Already a first-class road connects Dubai, Sharjah, and Ras al Khaimah. To this highway Ajman, Um al Quaiwain, and Digdagga are linked by excellent metalled roads. Between Abu Dhabi and Al Ain there is an impressive four-lane highway which has been constructed at a cost of 730,000 Dirhams a kilometre. Many new links have recently been completed or are in course of construction. Among those completed is a road between Abu Dhabi and Dubai, 132 kilometres in length. A coast road along the Batinah Coast, connecting Gufa, Kalba, Fujairah, Khor Fakkan, and Dibba, and an important trans-peninsular road between the Arabian Gulf and the Gulf of Oman have now been completed, though work on the latter progressed slowly, partly because of the difficulty of the terrain, especially through the Wadi Siji and the Wadi Ham, and partly because of financial difficulties. Yet another important link is being forged by the construction of a road along the coast of Abu Dhabi linking the capital with Tarif, Jebel Dhanna, and Al Sala, which eventually will be pushed on to Qatar, covering a distance of some 400 kilometres; from there it will connect with a trans-Arabian highway through Saudi Arabia. When this link is completed, the grand plan of road transport from the Gulf to Europe will have been achieved, and we shall have in being a modern counterpart to the dream of the Baghdad-Berlin railway, which was intended to terminate in Kuwait rather than in Baghdad and thus to link in easy and rapid communication the warm waters of the Gulf with the cold waters of the Baltic. When these international highways are completed a lorry from Manchester, Aberdeen, Bordeaux, Frankfurt, or Vienna will be able to travel all the way to Rams, Kalba, or Khor Fakkan, and with relays of drivers will be able to accomplish the journey in a matter of a few days. In addition to the coast road linking Abu Dhabi Town with Tarif, an inland road is being built commencing at Tarif and terminating in the Liwa area with a minor road to serve the Liwa villages.

Within the towns, roads have been vastly improved during the past few years. Many of these roads, as for example those in Abu Dhabi and in the congeries of villages which constitute Al Ain, have double carriageways and are fully lighted. Dubai, Sharjah, Ras al Khaimah, and even Ajman and Um al Quaiwain now all have good local roads, and in Dubai new bridges and a tunnel have been constructed to facilitate communications between the twin towns of Dubai proper and Deira.

With the improvement in the road system there has been a great increase in the number of motor vehicles, and in Abu Dhabi there is already about one motor vehicle for every four persons and the number of vehicles increases every year. Taxi cabs are numerous, and it is possible to obtain a cheap ride by sharing, since service taxis ply between the more popular centres. The service taxis provide cheap transport for inter-state travel between such centres as Dubai and Abu Dhabi, Sharjah, Ras al Khaimah, Al Ain, and even Oman. To purchase a ride all that is necessary is to go to some recognized centre where the long-distance taxis are waiting, each departing as soon as it is full. In 1974 there were 35,631 motor vehicles licensed in Abu Dhabi, and about 25,000 in Dubai.

AIR TRANSPORT

Air transport has done much to open up communications between the states and the outside world, and it has developed so greatly that it is now commonly used by all who can afford the cost. Air transport indeed has a relatively long history in Trucial Oman as it goes back to the early 'thirties. Sharjah was a staging post on Imperial Airways' route to India and the Far East. In 1932, Sharjah's Ruler signed an agreement with the air company which gave it permission to build a rest house for passengers and flying staff. In 1937 the Ruler of Dubai entered into a Civil Air Agreement which allowed Imperial Airways to establish a landing base on the creek for their flying boats. The Second World War put an end for the time being to civil aviation, but during that war Sharjah airfield was used by the RAF by agreement with the Ruler. After the war, the flying boat went out of use and the more powerful and longer-range aeroplanes of BOAC no longer needed either Sharjah or Dubai and tended to over-fly the old bases. Though they took a different form, air services remained important in the Gulf and rapidly developed when modern airports became available. The needs of the oil companies, including those engaged in prospecting and drilling as well as the producers, provided a basis of the demand for air transport services, and in 1950 a local air transport undertaking, known as Gulf Aviation, now Gulf Air, was formed to provide a regular network of air services in the area; in the following year, BOAC became a shareholder with a 51 per cent interest. The rest of the capital was provided by the governments of Bahrain and Qatar together with a number of private shareholders. The company from its beginning has sought to provide a high frequency of services between the Gulf states and also to serve the needs of the various oil companies prospecting or operating both off shore and on shore. In 1966, for example, Gulf Aviation flew a total of 159,121 miles on behalf of Abu Dhabi Petroleum Company and carried 5,644 tons of cargo for the company. Charter flights are provided as required for the oil companies, including flights by light aircraft for small party charters. A special feature of Gulf Aviation services has been the operation of "mercy flights" in cases of accidents involving physical injuries and in cases where urgent hospital treatment is needed. These flights have often been required at extremely short notice, and the company aims at having their aircraft airborne within thirty minutes of an emergency call. The pilots on such flights have when necessary landed their machines on small or improvised airstrips with only car headlights to illuminate the area for their landing and subsequent take-off.

There are three main airports serving the needs of the United Arab Emirates, apart from landing strips serving local needs or those of the oil companies, as on Das Island. The airports of Dubai and Abu Dhabi are up to full international standards and are capable of handling the largest jet planes. In 1974, Abu Dhabi Airport handled 435 thousand passengers, 11,121 tons of merchandise and 231 tons of air mail. Dubai Airport in the same year handled 739 thousand passengers and

11,614 tons of freight. Sharjah Airport, which is only three kilometres away from the centre of Sharjah Town, was built over thirty years ago, but since then the runway has been extended to a length of 7,500 feet with a width of 100 feet. Modern radar equipment has been installed and a new transit lounge has been constructed. A civil aviation school has been established near the airport, where instruction and facilities are available for all who desire them; it awards diplomas which are approved by British government authorities. A commercial "air taxi" service is available from the airport and this is extensively utilised by oil companies and other commercial firms. Sharjah and Dubai airports are separated by only a few miles and are connected by a good road. They are alternative calling points for local services, some flights going to the one and other flights to the other.

Dubai and Abu Dhabi International Airports are served by numerous airlines providing direct or scheduled connections with practically all the main capital cities of the world. At Dubai airport some 15,000 aircraft land or take off each year, and at Abu Dhabi's airport there are some 10,000 such aircraft movements. Passengers arriving at Dubai airport now number well over 200,000 a year, with approximately the same number departing. At Abu Dhabi airport about 150,000 arrive each year and about the same number depart. In addition to passenger traffic, there is also a considerable volume of traffic in merchandise for urgently required commodities, perishables, and mail, and to Dubai in gold. In 1974, some 7,000 tons of freight came in by air to Abu Dhabi and over 8,000 tons to Dubai. In 1975 a fourth large airport was opened in Ras al Khaimah.

PORTS AND HARBOURS

Adequate port facilities and efficient handling of cargoes are of fundamental importance to the United Arab Emirates, which depend on imports to feed, clothe, and maintain the standards of living of their populations, and on the export of oil to provide the means to pay for these imports. Large modern ports have recently been built in Dubai and Abu Dhabi, while smaller ports in Sharjah, Ras al Khaimah, and Khor Fakkan have been resuscitated and greatly improved. Oil terminals capable of loading the largest tankers have been constructed on Das Island and at Jebel Dhanna and more recently off shore in Dubai. Yet another oil terminal has just been built at the time of writing by the Abu Dhabi Oil Company (Japan) on an island named Halat al Mubarras, fifty-five miles west of Abu Dhabi Town.

Dubai Port

In the early years of the century, Dubai grew in importance as a trading centre, and it became a regular port of call from 1902 onwards for steamers serving the Gulf. Dubai bestrides a creek which runs some seven miles inland, the northern side of which is called Deira and the south Dubai. In 1957, a port development scheme was undertaken and the entrance channel through unstable sand bars was dredged, as was the creek itself, so providing a depth of from eight to twelve feet depending on the tides. The depth was suitable for small local craft, and great use was and still is made of the facilities available for these small boats which served neighbouring ports in Ras al Khaimah, Bahrain, Qatar, and other parts of the Gulf; but large ocean-going vessels had to anchor off shore and their cargoes had to be transhipped into lighters. These lighters, operated by Gray Mackenzie and Company over the twenty-four hours of the day, discharged their loads at wharves in the creek, which totalled some 4,000 feet in length. The facilities were comprehensive; one wharf for example was allotted to traffic in bags and sacks and to Bombay–Karachi cargoes; another was specialized to handle cement and timber traffic, yet another was a heavy-lift wharf. One wharf was in addition given to general cargoes carried to Dubai in coasting vessels drawing not more than nine feet of water at low tide.

As trade increased, it became an urgent matter to provide a modern port which could receive large vessels alongside and so eliminate the cost and time taken in transhipping by means of the lighters. A new port therefore has been constructed, named Port Rashid after Dubai's energetic and progressive Ruler. This is a deep-water harbour and provides facilities which could not possibly have been developed in the creek. It is situated on a bare coastline adjacent to and south-west of the entrance to the creek; the site was chosen because deep water is there found fairly near to the coast. Construction began in January 1968 on a scheme to provide nine deep-water berths, but in May 1969 the project was increased to provide fifteen deep-water berths, totalling 8,900 feet in length. Eight berths with adjacent transit warehousing and ample open-storage space were in full operation by the end of 1971, but construction was so well in advance of schedule that the port with its fifteen berths was in full operation before the end of 1972. The harbour area is enclosed by a main breakwater, 6,200 feet long, and a lee breakwater of rockfill construction, 8,100 feet in length. The breakwaters provide 275 acres of sheltered water and an entrance 600 feet wide. The dredged depth is thirty feet but this will later be increased to thirty-eight feet. Oil tanker berths are also to be built. The estimated cost of the scheme to completion is £24 million, and the necessary finance has been arranged through loans from Lloyds Bank and the BBME, backed by the Export Credits Guarantee Department of the British government.

Abu Dhabi Port

Abu Dhabi, unlike Dubai, has no sheltered creek, and before 1962 cargo had to be landed on the beach from the lighters which served the ships standing eight kilometres off shore. Some improvement was effected in handling the lighters when a small jetty was constructed at the north-east end of Abu Dhabi Island, but due to the shallowness of the waters near the shore all cargoes had still to be transhipped. This meant considerable costs and also long delays, so that the shipping companies imposed surcharges on cargo destined for unloading at Abu Dhabi. A number of the Conference Lines serving the Gulf also found it unremunerative to call at Abu Dhabi, and their cargoes had to be off-loaded at neighbouring ports and transhipped by small craft or else sent by road from Dubai. The position was becoming acute during Abu Dhabi's boom years, in 1968 and 1969, and so it was decided to construct a large modern port to handle the growing traffic. The construction of a port was first mooted in 1967, and a Canadian consulting firm designed an offshore harbour built in deep water with a causeway to the shore, but in 1968 this scheme was revised in favour of a more ambitious project for an inshore deep-water harbour. In the meantime a 1,500 feet lighterage wharf was built, and completed in May 1969, allowing the lighters to unload much more easily than before. The contract had been made in July 1968 for this wharf, which was designed to provide 500 metres of quayside and an apron five metres in depth. Time was an important factor, so the work was pushed ahead as rapidly as possible and the whole project was completed in under ten months. The material dredged to form the channel was deposited behind the apron and was subsequently surfaced so as to provide a storage area of nearly 150,000 square metres. The wharf was so designed as to be suitable for conversion later into three berths for the projected deep-water port.

The new harbour, which has been named Mina Zaid, when completed will have seventeen berths at which ships of up to nine metres draught will be able to tie up. This is sufficient depth for all general cargo ships at present operating in the Gulf, and they will be able to enter the harbour at all stages of the tides by a dredged channel some six kilometres long. The first stage of the construction of the port was completed in July 1972, when a breakwater of over three kilometres in length had been built, the channel dredged, and land reclaimed. Three deep-water berths and associated works were then completed and put into use. All the material for the breakwater and the retaining bank had to be imported from Ras al Khaimah, which involved the shipping of over a million tons of rock. Cargo landed at Mina Zaid amounted in 1974 to 582 thousand tons. Tankers are loaded with crude oil at the oil terminal ports of Jebel Dhana (ADPC), Das Island (ADMA) and Mubarris (ADOC Japan). In 1974, over 66 million tons of crude oil were shipped at these ports.

Sharjah Port

Sharjah's port, now known as Mina Khalid, has staged a remarkable come-back during the past few years. Sharjah was at one time the second largest commercial centre in the Gulf but fell on hard times in the 1930's and appeared until recently to many people as a somewhat somnolent "has been", especially as the port during the depression years had been allowed to silt-up. A project was initiated in 1959 to build a deep-water jetty and a breakwater, but these schemes had to be abandoned because of lack of funds. In 1965, however, work started on the construction of a 2,000 feet jetty with two berths for ships up to 10,000 tons. In 1969, a contract amounting to one million pounds sterling was awarded to a British firm, Tarmac Construction, for the cutting of a channel through the sandspit which forms the outer bank of Sharjah Creek, so that ships of up to one thousand tons could enter the lagoon. A berth for oil tankers has been constructed, a cold storage shed completed and a slipway provided for repair to fishing vessels. Work on further improvements to Port Khalid continues. Some commentators have pointed out that there are already two large ports in the UAE, but the authorities in Sharjah are firmly convinced that there is room for a third port, even though it is located only a short distance from Dubai. They point out that the offshore oil field is bringing new trade to the port and that even now ships have sometimes to wait their turn to use the other ports.

The Smaller Ports

There has been a revival of interest in the smaller ports and several of those which had decayed or become silted up have been taken in hand and improved. Ras al Khaimah, with the help of the Trucial States Development Fund and that of an American oil company, has now a new jetty and a breakwater. It can even boast a second port, at Khor Khowair, which will handle exports from a new cement factory which has been located nearby and which had originally been built to load barges with the stone required for Abu Dhabi's port construction.

On the other side of the Peninsula, the natural harbour of Khor Fakkan has been greatly improved and now presents a very tidy and workmanlike appearance. It has become a centre for fisheries research and development. Khor Fakkan in the past was an important port as it is the best natural harbour all the way between Cape Musandum in the north and Muscat in the south. In the 16th and early 17th centuries it was controlled by the Portuguese, then it was seized by the Persians in 1622, only to be re-conquered soon afterwards by an Arab force from Oman.

POSTAL SERVICES

The first post office in the Trucial States was established in 1909 in Dubai, which was even then an active trading centre with correspondents in many countries. The government of India was responsible for the service and overprinted Indian stamps were issued until October 1947. In that month, Indian stamps with a Pakistani overprint came into use when Pakistan took over the postal agencies in Dubai and Muscat. On 1 April 1948, British Postal Agencies, an organization linked to the GPO in London, assumed responsibility for the postal services in the Gulf countries of Dubai, Kuwait, Bahrain, Qatar, and Muscat. British stamps were put into circulation surcharged with rupee values (the rupee being the local currency in all these countries), but without any other distinguishing overprint. These stamps continued in use until 1959, when they were superseded in Dubai by a new set of Trucial States stamps sold through the post office there until 1963. These were pictorials depicting pearls, native sailing vessels, and date palms.

In 1963, the Ruler of Dubai took over the local postal services in his shaikhdom, and in the following year they were completely reorganized with the aid of a British Postal Officer seconded from the GPO, London.

British Postal Agencies opened a post office in Abu Dhabi in 1963, and at first used British stamps overprinted with rupee values. A special definitive issue of stamps for Abu Dhabi was later made depicting Shaikh Shakbut, which was used until the accession of Shaikh Zaid in 1966. Sharjah also started up a post office of its own in 1963, but was persuaded to use the services of a private company, the Middle East Stamp Company, which both printed and marketed the stamps. The shaikhdoms of Um al Quaiwain, Ajman, and Fujairah followed this example and concluded an agreement with the Barodi Stamp Company to run their services. Later, however, Um al Quaiwain and Ajman terminated this agreement and concluded another with J. H. Stanlow Inc. of New York.

By the year 1964, all the states were issuing stamps of their own. The sale of stamps, once initiated, was enthusiastically pursued by the smaller states and a regular spate of pictorial issues began to flow after 1964, covering all kinds of topical subjects ranging from commemoratives of President Kennedy and Winston Churchill to the Tokyo Olympic Games and the Centenary Stamp Exhibition in Cairo. Some of the themes selected, such as that of space research, would however appear to have little relevance to Trucial Oman. Perhaps it was hoped that philatelists might be attracted by the nature of the themes or by such novelties as the triptych issues of Sharjah, of which the side panels were of different values and could be detached, if desired, for separate use. Another novelty was a circular stamp embossed on silver foil to mark the occasion of the Arabian Gulf Monetary Conference in 1966. More relevant and more interesting were a design depicting a Sharjah street and wind-tower, and another depicting Kalba Castle.

In view of the small volume of postal traffic in some of the states, no doubt any contribution from stamp collectors would be doubly welcomed by the postal administration and the government. Abu Dhabi and Dubai, which had a genuinely busy postal service, were more restrained in their use of pictorials and the rule seems to have been the smaller the state, the more exotic its stamp issues.

Though home delivery of letters is available in some of the towns, the almost universal practice is to use post office boxes, which are the more necessary as houses do not have numbers and most streets do not have names. Those persons who do not have a post box of their own use that of a friend, their office, or a shop. Until recently it was also necessary to post all letters at the post office, but now posting boxes are being made available in many districts.

Professional letter writers sit outside the post offices at little tables and compose and write letters for the illiterate for a small fee. Theirs is an occupation of great antiquity in the Middle East.

Postal traffic is heavy in both Abu Dhabi and Dubai Towns and their postal services are very complete and efficient. In Abu Dhabi, for example, some $2\frac{1}{2}$ million letters or packets are posted in the year, and something like 2 million delivered. Inland letter post in Abu Dhabi was until 1973 charged at the very moderate rate of five fils, which is equivalent to about one new half-penny in Britain. It is now ten fils, but this rate also extends to letters sent to any other emirate in the Federation.

In Dubai about 4 million items of correspondence are posted in a year. In Ras al Khaimah, a postal service was introduced in 1964 and the services of the British Bank of the Middle East are utilized to provide the necessary facilities for holding stocks of stamps in safe deposit and issuing them as required to maintain counter stocks at the post office. A wide variety of stamps have been issued and some of these have been sold in the form of miniature sheets which it was hoped would attract philatelists and thus augment postal revenues.

After the formation of the United Arab Emirates, the postal services of all the seven states were on 1 August 1972 amalgamated under a single postal headquarters located in Abu Dhabi, which operates under the Federal Ministry of Communications. From that date, until the issue of a new series of stamps in 1973, the existing stamps were overprinted: UAE. Now the postal services are a federal service and all the seven emirates have stamps in common.

TELECOMMUNICATIONS

Telephone services are now available in all the emirates, managed and operated by Cable and Wireless Limited, by Abu Dhabi Telegraph and Telephone Company Limited, or by International Aeradio Limited (IAL). This latter company specializes in airport communications throughout the world and is entirely owned by the international airline undertakings. Cable and Wireless Limited provides telecommunications services in Sharjah, Ras al Khaimah, and Fujairah. The company also operates external radio communications for Dubai, but the internal telephone system is run by the Dubai State Telephone Company, of which Shaikh Rashid, the Ruler, is Chairman. The company, despite its name, is not a nationalized undertaking but is jointly owned by IAL and a group of local shareholders. The word "State" in its title simply indicates that it covers the emirate as a whole. It also extends its operations outside Dubai to Ajman and to Um al Quaiwain, for whose telephone systems it is the managing and operating company. Formed in 1959, the Dubai State Telephone Company includes under its management not only the telephone systems of Dubai, Ajman, and Um al Quaiwain but also the air traffic control and aeronautical telecommunications of Dubai's International Airport, together with the airport fire and rescue services. In 1971 a new electronic telephone exchange was installed, which, together with the older electro-mechanical exchanges, has a capacity of 7,000 lines. In comparison the telephone systems of Ajman and Um al Quaiwain are very small, though no doubt they will expand in the near future. In 1971 there were only eighty subscribers in Ajman and a mere sixty-nine in Um al Quaiwain.

In Abu Dhabi both the internal and external public telephone and telegraph services are provided by the Abu Dhabi Telegraph and Telephone Company Limited (ADTT), which was formed in 1962. The company is a joint enterprise with just over a third of its shares owned by IAL and the remainder by local shareholders. It does not, however, depend solely on its equity capital for financing its enterprises but is able to borrow on favourable terms from the banks and from merchant banking and other financial houses. ADTT has grown rapidly since 1967. In 1963 there were only fifty lines in use, and by 1967 the number had climbed to 500. By 1970 it had jumped to 1,900, in 1971 it reached 2,800, and by 1973 there were 5,201 lines in use. This last increase was made possible by the installation of a new electronic exchange in Abu Dhabi Town and another in Al Ain. Capacity in Abu Dhabi Town was raised to 3,500 lines and in Al Ain to 1,000 lines. The two exchanges, which are about 100 miles apart, are connected by an underground co-axial cable. The demand for telephone lines in Abu Dhabi Town has grown so rapidly that it has been difficult to meet all requirements at short notice, as extension of the service requires the laying of additional cables and the installation of more and ever larger exchanges.

International Aeradio has been entrusted in Abu Dhabi with full responsibility for air traffic control and for the operation and maintenance of the radio and navigation facilities of the International Airport. Among the services provided are those of a meteorological office which has been recording much-needed and valuable statistical data relative to meteorology since its formation in October 1970.

IAL, besides operating the technical services at the airport, provides communication systems for the oil companies working in Abu Dhabi. Under contract with the Abu Dhabi Petroleum Company (ADPC) it provides, operates, and maintains a comprehensive communications network for the company throughout the emirate. An ultra high frequency (UHF) communications system has been provided for the offshore oil company, Abu Dhabi Marine Areas (ADMA), linking their Zakum offshore platform with Abu Dhabi Town, some fifty miles distant. The oil terminal is also linked by radio to the town office.

Telex services are provided in Dubai and Sharjah by Cable and Wireless, and in Abu Dhabi by IAL. In Dubai such services have been available from 1968 and in Abu Dhabi from 1970. Both systems are on the International Telex System, which enables subscribers to contact any other subscriber in any part of the world. In Abu Dhabi, when telex services were introduced in 1970, there were 33 subscribers; by 1973 the number of subscribers had increased to 139, who made 70 thousand calls in the year.

International communication by telephone or cable is available from all the emirates, and the construction by Cable and Wireless of an earth station in Bahrain, to which the UAE is linked, has greatly facilitated and improved international communications.

On the Batinah Coast, Fujairah is the only centre with a telephone system, but it is very small, consisting of one exchange serving a few hundred subscribers. A telegraphic service, however, is provided from Khor Fakkan through Sharjah by means of a radio link operated by Cable and Wireless, but as yet there is no local telephone system there. Steps are now being taken to unify telecommunication services throughout the Federation.

From the foregoing review of the transport facilities and the communications network, it will be apparent that progress amounting to a revolution has been achieved in providing these important elements in the infra-structure of the Federation, which not only will provide for the future economic development of the individual emirates but should make an important contribution to the further economic and social integration of the area as a whole.

Chapter 12

Education

Under a ruling of the Federal Council, dated 29 June 1972, primary education in the Federation was made compulsory for all children over six years of age. Twenty years before, in 1952, there was not a single school in any of the seven shaikhdoms. Then the only education available was that provided in the *Kuttabs*, where groups of boys sitting in a circle and swaying backwards and forwards were taught to recite the Koran by a *mullah*, who might sometimes, though rarely, also teach his pupils to write. Owing to the lack of educational facilities in the past, the older people of the Federation are mostly illiterate, though not necessarily unintelligent. Usually they have good memories and can be shrewd in their judgement of character.

Education now in all the emirates has assumed a high priority, as it has come to be realized that their future development hinges largely on the rate at which nationals become qualified to assume responsibilities in government, administration, teaching, medicine, engineering, and industry. Unless nationals can be educated and trained to undertake these tasks, the states will have to rely for ever on expatriate skills and expertise. The problem is not one which is capable of a rapid solution, and therefore it is all the more necessary that attention should be given to devising educational systems which will have regard to the future pattern of needed skills. Something can of course be done in the short run by devising "crash courses" to combat illiteracy and innumeracy, as is being attempted for example in Abu Dhabi, but this is only a small though important part of the problem.

The original impetus to educational development was given by the governments of Britain and Kuwait, as the shaikhdoms lacked both the finance and the skills to set up modern education facilities on their own. Kuwait, having established her own educational system nearly twenty years before, began to give a helping hand to the then largely impoverished shaikhdoms of Trucial Oman, commencing with assistance to the first school, which had been established in 1953 in Sharjah. This school provided free education for 450 boys between the ages of six and seventeen. The school building was a gift of the British government, and the teachers were provided by the Kuwait Department of Education. For a long time, this was the only school in Trucial Oman to provide advanced courses as all the others subsequently inaugurated in the 'fifties provided only elementary education.

Sharjah not only has the distinction of being the first of the Trucial States to have had a school, but also proved herself most educationally minded in those pioneering days. In 1958 there were 520 pupils attending school in Sharjah. This may not seem to be a very great number for a population of about 25,000, as it then was, but it was somewhat more than half the total number of pupils at school in the seven states. Put in another way, Sharjah was educating somewhat more than 50 per cent of the children at school in the region, though she accounted for only about 12 per cent of the total population. Moreover, in those early days standards of education were higher in Sharjah than elsewhere in the area, as less reliance was placed on pure memory and on learning by rote—a common educational practice at that time in Arab education. In yet another aspect Sharjah was in the forefront of educational advance in the area, as she was the first state in Trucial Oman to provide educational facilities for girls, though admittedly the number receiving instruction was only seventy. In a highly conservative milieu, this must be regarded as a considerable achievement. Yet another distinction achieved by Sharjah in the educational field was the establishment of the first trade school. This was opened in November 1958, with one class of eighteen boys in training to become skilled artisans. A vocational school for the Trucial Oman Scouts was also inaugurated in Sharjah, with the aim of helping to fit the men for skilled employment after their discharge from the force.

After the successful inauguration of the first school in Sharjah, others were built by the British government in Ras al Khaimah, Abu Dhabi, and Khor Fakkan. In 1958, Kuwait also began to build schools, as for example in Ajman and Um al Quaiwain, and in subsequent years did much to bring educational facilities within the reach of the Gulf states. A special budget for the purpose was allotted by Kuwait, which in the scholastic year 1964–65 amounted to no less than half a million pounds sterling. Co-operation also came from Bahrain, Qatar, and the United Arab Republic (Egypt), all of which countries provided teachers, both men and women, free of cost to the shaikhdoms. Kuwait undertook the general supervision of education in all the shaikhdoms apart from Abu Dhabi, and each year the schools were inspected by Inspectors from the Kuwait Ministry of Education. The curriculum followed was that of Kuwait, and the subjects taught included the Koran, Arabic, arithmetic, history, geography, music, science, art and physical education. English was introduced at the intermediate level. School uniforms, books, stationery, school meals, and medical attention were provided for all children attending the schools at the expense of the Kuwait government. To facilitate administration a Kuwait Office was set up in Dubai, which also supervised the health services provided by Kuwait.

By 1964–65 there were thirty-one schools, apart from those in Abu Dhabi, which had its own systems of education and will be described later. Of these schools, twelve were for girls, with an attendance of 2,060. The boys' schools had 4,895 enrolled. The number of teachers was 301, and of these ninety-one were women. By 1967 the number of schools had increased to thirty-five and the total number of pupils to 10,549. Primary schools were operating in all the shaikhdoms, and post-primary education was available in Sharjah, Dubai, Ras al Khaimah, and Ajman. There were 412 teachers, of whom 269 were provided by the Kuwait government. The UAR provided eighty-six teachers, Qatar forty-two, Bahrain nine, while six were locally engaged and their salaries paid by the Rulers themselves. Though teachers' salaries were met by the donor state concerned, they were not necessarily nationals of the country. Many were Palestinians, Egyptians, or Lebanese. Out of the 412 teachers, 146 were women teachers working in the fifteen girls' schools open in 1967 and attended by 3,795 girls. This relatively large number of girls receiving education must be reckoned a considerable advance in an area where only a few years before there were no facilities at all for the formal education of girls. In 1967, there were primary schools for girls in all the shaikhdoms, including the smaller and less-developed of them, and girls' schools were also to be found in Kalba and Khor Fakkan, dependencies of Sharjah. There was, however, only one secondary school for girls, located as might be expected in Sharjah.

EDUCATION IN ABU DHABI

State education in Abu Dhabi dates back only to 1960/61, when three schools were opened. During this school year, 81 boys attended and were taught by six male teachers. Since then, the numbers of pupils and teachers have increased steadily, first at a moderate rate and then from 1967/68 at a very rapid rate. Schools for girls were introduced in 1963 and kindergartens, which are co-educational, in 1968.

By 1971/72 there were almost 11,000 pupils attending school, and by 1974/75 19,000 pupils were being educated in the government schools, taught by 1,098 teachers of whom 516 were women. In addition to the government schools there are a number of private schools, at which some 2,500 pupils are in attendance. Two are provided by the Catholic Mission and the others by various national communities, including British, American, Irani, Indian and French schools.

In 1971, it was calculated that 85 per cent of the children from six to eleven years of age were attending school. The percentage is now approaching 100 per cent.

Education in Abu Dhabi starts with the five-year-olds, and as elsewhere in the Federation it is entirely free. Abu Dhabi in addition pays a monthly stipend to all pupils attending the state schools, starting at 50 Dirhams a month (DH 40 for kindergarten pupils) rising to 150 Dirhams a month as the pupil progresses from grade to grade. These grants have now been extended to all the emirates. All books, stationery, drawing materials, and science laboratory materials are provided free, as are school meals and medical care. Two uniforms and one pair of shoes, as well as equipment for physical education and scouting, are issued to each child, and transport to and from schools is available free. Boarding houses are provided for children coming from remoter places and for those from other Gulf countries. In 1971/72, the two boarding houses, one in Abu Dhabi Town and the other in Al Ain, provided places for 812 students.

Kindergarten schools were started in 1968, and the number attending them rose to 1,114 in 1970 but fell off to seventy-six in the following year as the kindergarten premises were temporarily transformed into elementary schools to cope with a rush of entrants into the first-year elementary classes. A feature of educational development in recent years has been the opening of schools in remoter parts including Dalma Island, Yahar, Ramah, Al Khajnah and many others.

In addition to normal educational facilities for children and adolescents, there are also classes for adults who have not had the advantage of receiving adequate education in their youth. Many indeed never went to school and are completely illiterate. A special section of the Ministry of Education has been set up for combating illiteracy and promoting adult education. A sum of BD 30,000 was allocated to this sector in 1970 and the amount was increased to BD 40,000 in the following year.

In 1971–72 the number of persons attending the anti-illiteracy centres totalled 1,896, of whom ninety-three were females. Some of the students were fifty years old, though the majority were far younger, with about two-thirds under twenty-five. Most of the enrolments were in the Abu Dhabi Town and Al Ain centres, but the campaign against illiteracy is being extended to other areas, as for example Dalma Island and Bada Zayed. The number in attendance at the outlying centres was small, amounting to 127, but the numbers are growing as more and more centres are being opened each year.

Educational facilities for adults have been extended beyond those for illiterates, and the aim of the Ministry of Education is to provide evening classes for all adults who desire to continue their education from fifth primary through three years of preparatory (intermediate) classes right up to third year secondary. In 1971–72 there were 373 persons attending primary classes, of whom thirty-six were females; preparatory (intermediate) classes were attended by 111 persons, all of whom were males, and seventy-three joined the secondary classes. The number of centres is growing and adult educational facilities are being promoted for special groups of the population. A centre at Tarif has been set up for members of the police force stationed there, and special centres to serve members of the Abu Dhabi Defence Force (ADDF) have been formed in Abu Dhabi Town, Al Ain, and Al Hamra. The literacy and adult education classes are open freely to all persons whatever their nationality, and among expatriates it has been found that the courses are especially popular with Omanis. Throughout the Federation in 1974 there were 91 centres for adult education attended by 8,663 students.

EDUCATION IN DUBAI

In Dubai, as in Abu Dhabi, great stress is laid on the provision of educational facilities as a means of promoting the future prosperity and development of the emirate. Initially the impetus to education was fostered by the government of Kuwait, which financed the buildings and met the annual costs of running the schools and paying the teaching staff until the schools were taken over by the Federation. There are now about 3,000 pupils attending the government schools in Dubai, which offer a complete range of elementary, intermediate, and secondary education for both boys and girls. One of the schools provides a training course for teachers, and another has evening classes for those who have missed earlier attendance at day school. The Technical and Trade School, opened in 1964, offers four-year courses in carpentry and cabinet-making and in engineering. The engineering curriculum is designed to prepare students for the City and Guilds examinations, and the subjects which can be studied include motor vehicle repair and maintenance, electrical installation work, engineering fitting, machine shop work, welding, and fabrication. Successful students can follow their studies with a further two-year secondary course, specializing in one or other of the engineering subjects, or in carpentry and cabinet-making. A business studies course is also available for those students who have completed their intermediate education in general subjects.

In accord with Dubai's reputation for following liberal policies, foreign residents in Dubai are encouraged to build and run their own community schools. Among such schools already established, the largest is the Iranian School, which is financed by the government of Iran and is inspected at regular intervals by representatives of the Iranian Ministry of Education. The courses available in this school cover primary, intermediate, and secondary levels, and the curriculum is based on that followed in Iran. About 600 boys and 300 girls attend the school, but the demand for places is so great that the school is being forced to expand its facilities. There are also an English-speaking school, an American Community School, and a Pakistani Middle School, which is Urdu-speaking and co-educational. There is an Indian primary school and the National Private School, which is fee-paying and run as a private enterprise, teaching Arabic, French, and English to children whose parents intend that they should later continue their education in the Lebanon.

SCHOOLS IN THE OTHER EMIRATES

As previously mentioned, Sharjah has long been in the forefront of educational advance, but it is only recently that the other northern emirates have begun to expand their educational activities. In Ras al Khaimah, when the first elementary school was opened in 1955, the numbers of pupils, all boys, was only about 200, but by 1971 the number of schools had been increased to twenty-six and the number of pupils to 5,200, with facilities for both boys and girls up to and including secondary classes. Employment of young persons under eighteen years of age is prohibited, in order to induce children and young persons to attend school. Free transport is available for those living some distance from their school, and all books and materials as well as two uniforms a year are provided free. A trade school and an agricultural school afford specialized instruction and there is an institute specializing in religious studies, law, and jurisprudence. Higher education is encouraged by the provision of scholarships to various universities abroad, including Kuwait, Amman, Damascus, Beirut, Cairo, and London Universities.

In the smaller shaikhdoms of Ajman, Um al Quaiwain, and Fujairah, educational facilities have been increasing with help from Kuwait and other countries. In the United Emirates as a whole, 55,000 children were receiving formal education in 1975.

TRAINING COURSES

The contributions made by the oil companies in Abu Dhabi by providing training facilities for craftsmen and technicians have been of the greatest importance in producing a nucleus of skilled workers. A sizeable number of ex-trainees are now engaged in skilled jobs both inside and outside the oil industry.

Physicians, chartered engineers, teachers, architects, chemists, hydrologists, lawyers, administrators, and a host of other specialists are required in increasing numbers in the Gulf states, but so also are artisans, craftsmen, and technicians. Facilities for training in the crafts are equally essential, as are those for teaching future professional men, if a developed well-balanced economy utilizing native talents is to be achieved. The old crafts of ship-building, weaving, pottery, and wood-carving are disappearing, and in their place a new generation of workers skilled in the engineering and building trades, in electrical installation, motor vehicle maintenance, metal working and the like is required and needs to be trained.

The "new look", however, requires a change in outlooks. To own and tend a herd of camels, to own and run a taxi, to drive a lorry, to teach, to administer a government department, to conduct an import or export business, to be a policeman or a night watchman, carries each in its own sphere a certain kudos, but as yet the artisan skilled in the requirements of the new technology—the welder, the cable jointer, the horticulturist, the sheet-metal worker—has not attained the status which he deserves in the economies of the Gulf.

THE TRADE SCHOOLS

Some reference has already been made to the trade schools of Sharjah, Dubai, and Ras al Khaimah, as it is in the field of education and training that most help has been given to the Trucial States over recent years. The trade schools were originally designed to train artisans, and from their inception the policy of accepting only nationals of the Trucial States has been followed except for some students coming from Oman. The standard of entry has gradually been raised. The first students in 1958 were without primary education and had to be taught to read and write, but as outside facilities improved, standards of entry could be raised, and by 1964 all entrants were literate in Arabic and a full four years of primary education became a required qualification for entry to the trade schools. The scope of the schools was also extended to cover a planned programme of technical teacher-training, and ex-students selected for such training were sent abroad for further study in Khartoum, Kuwait, Bahrain, or Beirut. From 1965 onwards selected ex-students were sent to the United Kingdom, where a link was established with the Crawley College of Further Education and also with King Alfred's College, Winchester.

The policy of providing teaching staff from among local people as soon as possible was laid down in the early days of the Sharjah school.

The original building at Sharjah consisted of two small workshops and an office, but new workshop blocks and classrooms were gradually added. In 1960–61, the total number of students in training was thirty, of whom seventeen were being trained in carpentry and thirteen in motor maintenance. By 1964 there were forty-eight students under training; the number of teachers and instructors had risen to eight, and all the courses included classes in Arabic, English language, mathematics, and engineering drawing.

In the meantime it was decided to build a second trade school at Deira in Dubai. This was in 1962, before the metalled road connecting Sharjah to Dubai had been built, and it was difficult for students from Dubai to make the double journey each day to and from Sharjah. The framework of the new buildings for the Dubai trade school was erected by a contractor under the supervision of the school staff, but the roofs, the doors, and the timber and metal fittings were all made by the students of the Sharjah trade school, who also carried out the electrical installation work. This was in effect a kind of communal "do-it-yourself", and served to give the students a worthwhile exercise in practical work.

The Dubai Trade School was opened in January 1964, with thirty-six students attending three-year courses in mechanical engineering, carpentry and cabinet-making, or in electrical installation work. All the students had completed a minimum of three years' primary education before enrolment. In that year also this entrance standard was enforced at the Sharjah school and the length of the previous two-year courses was extended to three years.

The Dubai Trade School made good progress, and two years after its opening a commercial course was introduced extending over three years with an annual intake of fifteen students. The curriculum covers Arabic and English typing, mathematics and accounting, office practice and procedures, commercial law, commercial geography, and business administration. These commercial courses for local students are a specially valuable contribution to the needs of Dubai with its intensive business activities.

The entrance standard set for the commercial course is higher than any previously required by the trade schools, as the commercial students are required to have completed eight years' previous education.

The technical courses provided in both Sharjah and Dubai Trade Schools allow for specialization in any one of four fields, namely general engineering, motor vehicle maintenance, carpentry and cabinet-making, and electrical installation work.

There are thirty teaching hours a week and of these fourteen are spent in the workshops and sixteen in classroom studies. All students now include in their studies Arabic, English, mathematics, engineering drawing, general science, and social studies.

A third trade school was opened in September 1969 in Ras al Khaimah, and the technical courses given there are very similar to those in Sharjah.

The latest development in the trade school courses up to the time of writing was the starting in September 1971 of a secondary technical course in Dubai requiring a higher entrance qualification and leading to advanced City and Guilds examinations.

In the trade schools in Sharjah and Dubai standard lesson notes have been prepared by the staff and are provided for the use of each student. The notes become the property of the student and are a valuable work of reference which has proved useful not only during the course but afterwards, when the graduated student is working in industry on his own without the guidance of his tutors. They also serve as useful guides to those young instructors who are gradually taking over the work of training their own compatriots.

In the school year 1971–72 the total number of trainees attending the trade schools was 386, of whom Dubai claimed 244, Sharjah eighty, and Ras al Khaimah sixty-two. These would not be regarded as large numbers in a western developed country but they are a valuable contribution to the development of the United Arab Emirates.

Abu Dhabi has been a late starter in the field of government-sponsored technical education, but a new technical school commenced work at the end of 1972. In Abu Dhabi the need for a trade school like those in Sharjah or Dubai has not in the past been so urgent because of the facilities provided by the training schools of the two oil companies. It has unfortunately to be recorded that attendance at the various vocational schools has not increased along with those attending other courses, and indeed has fallen off from a peak in 1971.

THE GULF TECHNICAL COLLEGE

At the apex of technical education in the Gulf is the Gulf Technical College, located in Bahrain, which was set up by the Rulers of Bahrain and Abu Dhabi with the assistance of the British government. The Rulers of the other Gulf states were consulted before the college was established and they welcomed the project as a potential contribution of great value to the development of the area. The Ruler of Bahrain, Shaikh Isa, donated a site of fifty acres just south of Isa Town and provided various access facilities. The Ruler of Abu Dhabi and the British government each contributed half of the capital costs and initially half of the recurrent costs. The college opened in 1969 and set for itself as its aim the training of school-leavers from any of the Gulf states in higher technical skills than can be provided within the scope of the educational systems in individual states. Courses are given in technical and advanced trade subjects, in commercial and business studies, and in public administration. Students are prepared for external examinations such as those of the City and Guilds or the Royal Society of Arts. In this way it is hoped to maintain a high standard by enabling students to qualify in objective tests held by impartial, outside bodies whose qualification awards are well known and trusted.

ADMA TRAINING CENTRE

As part of its policy of helping nationals from Abu Dhabi to make a career for themselves in the oil industry, Abu Dhabi Marine Areas Ltd (ADMA) established a training scheme in 1959 to train Abu Dhabians on the job, whereby they might gain the necessary experience to enable them to take on greater responsibilities and eventually be capable of replacing expatriate employees in technical and administrative departments. A training centre was also established and a building to house the centre was erected on a site near the company's head office. This centre, which was officially opened on 22 March 1961, provides both academic and practical training in technical and commercial subjects.

Starting with eight students who were trained on plant operation in the power house, the training centre gradually increased admissions to thirty a year, all of them nationals of Abu Dhabi or the other emirates. After completing two years at the training centre, the trainees are sent to Das Island for on-the-job training, during which they attend day-release classes one day a week and evening classes, each of two hours' duration, on two days a week.

Those students attending the training centre whose homes are outside Abu Dhabi Town are accommodated at a hostel which can provide facilities for sixteen students. Students whose progress warrants it are sent for further study either to the Gulf Technical College in Bahrain or to the United Kingdom, where those with a sufficient academic background attend a three-year degree course at Swansea University; others attend National Diploma Courses at Neath Technical College or can be assigned to the BP Research Centre at Sunbury. During their courses in Dubai or in Bahrain, students are encouraged to sit for external examinations such as those of the Royal Society of Arts in Commerce, or the City and Guilds Engineering GI and GII examinations.

While training, the students are placed on the company's payroll with attractive rates of pay, which are increased as a student progresses through his course. At the end of 1971, the company was training seventy-four nationals between the ages of fifteen and thirty, either in the training centre or on the job at Das Island, at the Gulf Technical College or in the United Kingdom.

ADPC TRAINING CENTRE

Abu Dhabi Petroleum Company began to provide training facilities in Tarif almost as soon as oil production got under way. Later the centre was moved to Abu Dhabi Town, where a special building has been provided, equipped with administrative offices, classrooms, workshops, and language laboratories, together with facilities for the staff and the students.

Since its inception the centre has concentrated on providing training for carefully selected nationals in various technical crafts and in commercial subjects. The numbers completing the courses in any one year have not been very large, but the cumulative total over the years has been impressive in terms of local conditions, and the centre has made an important contribution in providing the country with skilled workers from among its own nationals. Not all the graduated trainees have remained with the oil company itself, but this has been regarded by the company as part of its contribution to the general welfare of the emirate. In 1971, there were thirty-nine Abu Dhabian employees undergoing training for technical and clerical posts. Twenty-six were attending full-time classes at the training centres. These trainees were entered for recognized examinations, and selected candidates took the examinations of the Royal Society of Arts in English, commercial arithmetic, and typing. Others successfully completed the first year of the General Engineering Course of the City and Guilds. Eight trainees were engaged in full-time training on the job, within the company organization.

In September 1972 an important development took place when an apprenticeship scheme for Abu Dhabi nationals was grafted onto the previous training scheme and the students already in attendance were transferred to the new scheme so as to avoid any break in continuity. The objectives of the Apprenticeship Course are stated to be, firstly, the training of nationals towards intermediate and senior positions in the company, and, secondly, the training and development of nationals to the limit of their potential so as to enable them to meet the full requirements of operating posts within the company, and to replace expatriate employees in the shortest possible time. There is no contractual obligation on the trainees to remain with the company for a prescribed number of years, as the company recognizes that the training would be valuable outside the company and that some of those completing that apprenticeship course will be attracted to outside enterprises. This would enhance the prestige of the course and be of general benefit, though perhaps in a narrow view a loss to the company.

The training programme, which is of five years' duration, is divided into two main sections, one technical and the other commercial. For all, there is formal instruction in English and mathematics. Then those who opt for the technical programme study science, technology, technical drawing, and workshop practice. For the commercial apprentices the subjects include office practice, business administration, book-keeping and accounts, and typewriting. All candidates for admission to the apprenticeship courses must have completed their primary school education, be at least fourteen years of age, and must pass an entrance examination. The applicant must also be approved by the Ministry of Labour and Social Affairs and by the Ministry of Education. On the successful completion of the course, the apprentices are awarded a Certificate of Apprenticeship.

An apprentice who completes the academic work to a high standard and obtains external examination certificates which would enable him to satisfy entry requirements for courses of further education in the UK or other countries may be invited to join the company's Technical Professional Development Scheme for the Advancement of Nationals, as a company employee.

Chapter 13

Health and Housing

Though the climate is harsh in summer, the United Arab Emirates are not unhealthy apart from the usual respiratory afflictions during the winter season when temperatures are markedly changeable. Malaria, however, is endemic and widespread in the mountains and the Batinah coastal area, but occurs only occasionally in the larger towns. The health record of expatriates in Abu Dhabi and Dubai is good, as they are mostly young and active persons of between twenty and forty years of age.

There is now a nucleus for a complete medical service throughout the Federation, with excellently equipped hospitals in all the larger centres of population, including Abu Dhabi, Dubai, Sharjah, Ras al Khaimah, and Dibba. Clinics have been set up in most of the small towns and medical services are being extended to the villages by the opening of rural clinics or by means of motorized travelling clinics.

The provision of health services in the Trucial States dates back to 1949, when the British government decided to donate a hospital in Dubai and appointed Dr D. G. McCaully of the Indian Medical Service to start up a medical service and to take charge of the hospital. Further help in setting up medical services then came from several other quarters, including Kuwait (whose contributions have been described in a previous chapter), American missionaries, and the Trucial States Development Fund.

American Mission Hospitals have been opened in three of the emirates. The first was established in 1952 in Sharjah and the second, ten years later, in Al Ain, which is staffed by both American and Canadian missionaries. The third American Mission Hospital has been active for several years in Ras al Khaimah.

The Trucial States Development Office from its inception concentrated much of its activities in promoting health services, on which the expenditure was greater than on almost any other item up to the time its work was transferred to the Federation Ministries. It was particularly active in bringing medical services to outlying districts; it established clinics in Dhaid, Abu Musa, Sha'am, Digdagga, Jezirat Za'ab, Idhen, Masfut, and Haweilat.

Yet another source of aid has been the Iranian Red Lion and Sun Society, an Iranian equivalent of the Red Cross or Red Crescent Societies. This society runs a 150-bed hospital in Jumeriah in Dubai, which is very well equipped and designed. It is staffed entirely by Iranian physicians and nurses but serves patients of every nationality, not only in Dubai but also in branch hospitals in Ajman and Ras al Khaimah.

Private hospitals are also provided by the oil companies and the Defence Forces for their own personnel.

HOSPITALS

Dubai especially is well provided with medical services and hospitals. In addition to the Iranian Hospital there is a 60-bed hospital on the Deira side of the creek and a clinic on its Dubai side, which were provided and maintained by Kuwait until their recent transfer to the state. The Dubai government's own Al Maktum Hospital, which was completed in 1966, has over 100 beds. Recently a new hospital known as the Rashid Hospital has been opened, which has 393 beds, soon to be increased to 700 beds. The main building is fully air-conditioned and oxygen gas outlets are provided for a large number of the beds. This is a very modern hospital complex, with all necessary laboratories and specialized pathological, physio-therapy, and X-ray departments, as well as staff accommodation and a nursing school, together with kitchens, laundry facilities and other ancillary services. The staff for the hospital has been recruited from all over the world, but most of the nurses come from India, as in some Arab countries the emancipation of women has not yet progressed sufficiently for them to be employed in male wards. Dental treatment is available at the Kuwait and Iranian Hospitals, and a dental clinic is to be set up in Rashid Hospital.

In Abu Dhabi, medical services have developed rapidly since 1967, when there was but one government hospital of fifty beds in Abu Dhabi Town and the American Mission Hospital in Al Ain. The government in that year employed eleven physicians, and another seven were working in private practice. Two years before, there had been only one government physician and only three were in private practice.

By 1970 a 150-bed hospital had been built in Abu Dhabi Town and a twenty-five-bed government hospital in Al Ain. During that year there were over 3,500 admissions to the government hospitals. Female patients outnumbered males by some 400, but they stayed in hospital for only seven days on average, compared with eleven days for the male patients. Attendances at government out-patient clinics totalled 218,000 visits, and in addition nearly 88,000 patients attended private clinics. The number of medical practitioners including dentists had increased to sixty-eight by 1970.

Government dental services were first provided in Abu Dhabi in January 1968 within the framework of the Health Department, and in the following year over

10,000 patients underwent dental treatment. Mobile dental clinics have been imported from Britain and are used to provide dental services for schools in out-lying areas as part of a campaign to improve the health of children.

In Ras al Khaimah a government hospital was opened in 1963 and there are now three hospitals in the emirate, namely the Al Nakhil Hospital, provided by the government, the Kuwait Hospital, and the American Mission Hospital. Mobile clinics tour the villages on regular circuits to treat the sick, dispense medicines, and give medical advice. Hospital and medical treatment are provided free of charge to all Arab nationals and for patients in hospital there are free meals.

On the Batinah Coast there is a large modern hospital at Dibba. In Fujairah, there is a clinic but as yet no hospital. Sharjah has a large clinic staffed by four physicians and in Kalba there is a health centre which serves the surrounding area as well as Kalba Town. In Um al Quaiwain, the Abu Dhabi Department of Health has supervised the construction, furnishing, and equipment of a hospital which has been financed by Shaikh Zaid, the Ruler of Abu Dhabi, from his own personal funds.

Throughout the Federation, simple lessons in hygiene and nutrition are being given in the schools, and this teaching should in time do much to raise health standards throughout the area. Gradually also the old-fashioned "cures", nostrums, and superstitions are being ousted; and this trend is of especial importance in connection with midwifery and child care, where harmful practices were, and still are to some extent, all too common. A major survey of the medical requirements of the emirates is under way and it is expected that this will provide a detailed guide to future development.

HOUSING

Modern houses in the emirates are built either of cement blocks for bungalows or villas, or of reinforced concrete for multi-storeyed apartment and office blocks. Stone-built houses are confined to those areas such as Ras al Khaimah where stone is to be found, but, as might be expected, there is no tradition of stone buildings in the desert areas; there, even castles and fortresses were built of mud-brick. Many of the houses, amounting to some 40 per cent in the Federation, are flimsy structures of the *barasti* type, which are constructed from date-palm branches. Usually, except in some towns where space is limited, the *barasti* has a courtyard in front bounded by a *barasti* fence and consists of one or two rooms. Occasionally there may be five or six rooms or even more, but this is unusual, and more than half the *barastis* have one room only. Generally, however, there is no overcrowding, as extra rooms can easily be built or a new *barasti* may be erected should the household increase in size. *Barastis* have compacted sand floors and normally lack such services as electricity, piped water, or sewerage. The walls of a *barasti*, unlike those of concrete houses, do not retain the heat and therefore cool down much more rapidly after sunset. *Barastis* are especially numerous in Fujairah, where, according to the Population Census of 1968, 80 per cent of the houses were of this type. The trend now through-out the Federation is towards the replacement of the *barasti* by more permanent types of house, and in Abu Dhabi between 1968 and 1971 the percentage of stone or concrete houses increased fourfold while the number of *barastis* fell by 20 per cent. This is a measure of the great changes which have taken place in the emirate especially in the towns.

Not all houses however are of stone, concrete, or *barasti*, and in the 1968 census nearly 5,000 dwellings were enumerated as being of "other types". These other types included mud-brick houses, tents, boats, and, in the mountains of Ras al Khaimah, even caves.

In the larger towns, notably Abu Dhabi and Dubai, the trend is towards the erection of large blocks, centrally air-conditioned and rising four or more storeys. These blocks usually have shops or offices on the ground floor with the apartment flats confined to the upper storeys, which are generally served by lifts. Land in Abu Dhabi is owned by the Ruler, but he has allocated plots to nationals who have requested such property. On acquiring a title to a piece of land, a national may erect residential or commercial buildings on it, but he may not put up industrial structures without special permission, as there is now a scheme to zone the uses of land. A national can sell or exchange his plot for another piece of land subject to the Ruler's consent. Such transfers may only be effected with another national since non-nationals are not permitted to own land. Non-nationals are allowed to lease land from a national for the purpose of development and management. Such leases are subject to a maximum period of eight years, after which the land together with any buildings or improvements effected by the tenant revert to the original owner. It is also possible for an owner to reclaim the land with buildings and improvements made by the tenant after four years subject to any pre-determined compensation. In Dubai the position is much the same except that lease periods may extend to 20 years.

The short leases, especially in Abu Dhabi, have obvious drawbacks, in that tenants are reluctant to improve or even fully maintain the properties especially towards the end of the period of the lease. It would seem desirable that some form of tenant right should be devised providing compensation for improvements, if the city is not soon to develop areas of neglected and dilapidated structures. Even as it is, owners themselves are not fully aware of the importance of regular and early maintenance.

For the lower-income families, a considerable number of one-storey low-cost houses have been erected by the governments, including those of Ajman and Um al Quaiwain. These two towns in consequence are now looking less picturesque than they used to do some five or six years ago, but, in compensation, the inhabitants are much better housed and have modern amenities such as piped water and electricity laid on for them. Altogether in the northern emirates, 3,580 state-built houses had been provided for low income families by March 1974, and similar construction is still proceeding. In Abu Dhabi more than 3,000 low-cost houses have been constructed by the government and have been allocated free to Abu Dhabi nationals with limited incomes. Other Abu Dhabi nationals have been given a building plot free of charge on which to build a house of their own. Bedouins are being settled in those parts of their desert area where agricultural development is possible. Nine such settlements have been initiated and permanent houses erected for local Bedouins. Pumps have been installed to provide both drinking water and irrigation water for vegetable plots.

Large mud-brick houses were never numerous in Abu Dhabi Town, and few of the older houses, large or small, have been left standing in the rush towards modernization, and the last of the wind-towers has disappeared. In Dubai and Sharjah such houses built by rich merchants were more usual and a good number have survived, many of them with delightfully designed wind-towers still standing. These wind-towers, it is said, were introduced about 100 years ago by merchants from Iran. The older part of Dubai, located on the south side of the creek, maintains its traditional look, but on the other side, called Deira, a modern town has arisen with numerous multi-storeyed offices and flats. Neither in Abu Dhabi nor in Deira has there been any development of the flamboyant type of large mansions such as are to be found in Kuwait. All the large houses so far constructed are much more restrained in their architecture.

The black goat-hair tents of Bedouin nomads are still to be seen in the desert areas, but gradually the tribes are being settled and soon, it would seem, the Bedouin tent will be a thing of the past. These tents are well adapted to the nomadic way of life, as they are easily erected, dismantled, and transported on the backs of camels. They are low-lying and seem to hug the ground, being scarcely six feet high, and the side flaps can be raised to allow any cooling breeze there may be to pass through the tent. Like the *barasti*, they are surprisingly cool, that is in terms of the high temperatures prevailing outside during a summer's day. Again like the *barasti*, the walls do not act as heat accumulators as do those of concrete houses. But, lacking all modern conveniences and amenities, they have outlived their day.

As regards public buildings, mosques are to be found in all the towns and villages; each has a minaret or two, from which the call to prayer is made. Most are of simple mud-brick construction, though the more modern are often of concrete, and most are whitewashed. The Kuwait State Office in Dubai provided assistance for the building of mosques in small villages. In Abu Dhabi Town there is a splendid new mosque with two towering minarets and capable of accommodating several thousand worshippers. Two new small mosques stand out among many others recently completed as they are highly ornate and decorated in many striking colours, displaying the exotic influence of countries east of the Gulf.

Though the emirates are Moslem states, there is complete freedom of religious opinion and there are three Christian churches in Abu Dhabi Town: Catholic, Anglican, and Orthodox. Their congregations are of many nationalities, though among them Indian Christians predominate. There is a Catholic Chapel of Ease in Al Ain and also a church of the American Mission Hospital. In Dubai, a Catholic Church was opened in 1967 on land donated by Shaikh Rashid, the Ruler. This church is of modern design, circular in shape and with a central pinnacle-type tower. In Abu Dhabi also, the land for the churches was donated by the Ruler, Shaikh Shakbut.

Among other public buildings, the most prominent and interesting are the old forts and palaces, dating back to the last century or before. Notable examples are to be seen in Abu Dhabi Town, Al Ain, Kalba, Um al Quaiwain, and Ajman. They are of mud-brick construction, whitewashed, and usually with crenellated round or square towers.

Town-planning departments have been established in both Abu Dhabi and Dubai, and town plans have been made for Ras al Khaimah and Sharjah. The plans provide for the building of modern road systems (now practically completed in Abu Dhabi) with numerous roundabouts to facilitate traffic flow, for the zoning of the urban areas into residential, industrial, commercial, and other zones, and for the selection of suitable sites for schools, playing fields, and parks. In Abu Dhabi special attention is being given to planting the roundabout centres and the roadsides with grass, flowers, and shrubs. These efforts have been most successful and have done a great deal to relieve the drab monotony of the grey sands on which the town is built. In Dubai, though many old buildings have been demolished, special efforts are being made to preserve the essential character of the old town.

Social Welfare Benefits

In Abu Dhabi, generous assistance is provided for those nationals in need of help: such as widows, blind persons, or those otherwise incapacitated. In 1973 for example nearly twenty million Dirhams was distributed in social benefits to some four thousand families in need of assistance.

Chapter 14

Customs and Pastimes

Among Gulf nationals, society is largely traditional and conservative, especially in the rural and desert areas, with emphasis on religion, hospitality, good manners, and courtesy. Women go veiled and masked and are not to be seen at public gatherings. Even the shopping is largely done by the menfolk. The modern tendency, however, is towards greater freedom for women, and as the economies progress, this is likely to become increasingly the rule. Factors making for a new age are the education of girls and the introduction of television into so many households in the towns.

The serving of coffee in small handle-less cups is still the traditional form which hospitality takes; the coffee being freshly ground and made and flavoured with cardamom. It is served by the coffee-maker from long-beaked coffee pots, and traditionally it is polite to take up to three cups, fewer if one so wishes, and after one is satisfied one shakes the cup to indicate that no more is required. The coffee cup must be handed back to the server; it is considered rude to put it down. It is usual for the principal guest to be served first. He will, however, indicate with a slight wave of the hand that the host should take precedence, but on the host's declining, the guest then accepts. Coffee is served on all occasions: in the Ruler's *majalis* (reception room), in the home, in the office, maybe even in a shop. The coffee-server will have several cups and will pass on from one guest to the next, usually in clockwise fashion though sometimes first to the right and then to the left in succession. Having poured out all his cups, the server will return to the first guest to give a second or third helping. The host will be the last to be served. Any qualms which a westerner may have about drinking from the same cup as others will have to be forgotten, as when a guest finishes his cup it is refilled for another guest.

Meals tend to be of gargantuan size; possibly a whole lamb will be served on a great dish on a mountain of rice, and there will undoubtedly be many other dishes of chicken, fish, salads, and prepared delicacies. One eats with the right hand only;

never on any account with the left, but one's hand will have been washed before the meal by a servant who pours water over one's hand on entry to the dining place and provides a towel for drying. The meal is usually eaten very quickly and silently, and guests may rise and leave before the host rises. They return to the room where they had assembled for coffee. Incense and rosewater are traditional, and are dispensed before the guests leave. Rosewater is poured from a silver shaker by a servant, and the incense is carried round to each guest in a kind of thurible; the practice is to waft the incense smoke with one's right hand towards one's beard or chin. After coffee is served, guests take their departure. To the westerner these departures may seem to be rather abrupt, with just a bare good wish or thank you: it is on entry that the compliments are passed, and they can be very gracious. Food is always provided in overabundance, and much is left over. It is not wasted in the traditional household, as it will next be partaken of by the host's family, then by the servants, and any still left over will be distributed among the poor at the gate. Though this description applies to the large house and the important host, exactly the same procedures are followed even by the most humble host, though the scale and variety of the fare are different and the incense and the rosewater may be absent.

On entering a dwelling place, even though it be but a *barasti* or a tent, it is customary and polite to leave one's shoes outside. Generally there are no chairs and all sit cross-legged on the ground, but care must be taken not to point the soles of one's feet towards any other person.

Many old customs and traditions are still preserved in the emirates. Life is still uncomplicated except in the larger towns, and time does not press so hard as it does in the West. Much, however, is changing, and the traditional ways of life, together with their age-long customs, are giving way before the onslaught of social and economic change.

Among the traditional customs is the dance. Dancing figures prominently in celebrations such as those during the *Eids* (feast-days) and on special occasions such as circumcisions. The dances are performed with great gusto and skill to rhythmic drumming and the clash of cymbals. Only men participate, and in some of the traditional dances all the menfolk take part, rich and poor, old and young, ranging themselves in two lines facing inwards towards the musicians and leaders, who remain in the centre encouraging all to greater energy. Other dances are performed with swords waving in the air, celebrating perhaps some long-past tribal victory. Not infrequently the celebrations are enlivened by the dancers twirling their ancient muzzle-loading guns, which they discharge from time to time and then reload with gunpowder and ram-rod, still moving in time with the dance music. The leader provides them from time to time with a small handful of gunpowder without any interruption of the dance. For this dance, which is known as *Ardha*, the music is provided by large tambourine-like drums. A small fire is kept going to heat the drum-skins from time to time so that they will remain taut. In another dance, the *Laywah*, the music is provided by a long horn and a big drum vigorously beaten at intervals; this dance is much favoured by expatriate Omanis and Arabs of African descent. In yet another dance, imported from Arabistan and known as the *Jerbah*, the musical accompaniment is played on a bagpipe made from an inflated goatskin.

Singing is also traditional in the Gulf, not only during the feasts but also at work. In the past, on the sailing vessels engaged in long-distance voyages or in pearling expeditions, entertainment as a relief from monotony took the form of singing, with the music supplied by members of the crew. The songs are in very much the same tradition as our western sea-shanties, though more related to loved ones and families ashore. They were accompanied by drums and other musical instruments, including a pottery vessel played by cupping a hand over its mouth in rhythmic fashion to produce a musical sound through compression of the air within. There is also a tradition preserved to the present day among Omani sailors of singing in unison when performing tasks requiring co-operation or team-work either at sea or in port, when engaged for example in cleaning and scouring the hull of their ship.

THE SHIHUH

Though numerically not very numerous, the Shihuh of Ras al Khaimah have very different customs and traditions from the rest of the inhabitants of the United Arab Emirates, and are therefore of considerable anthropological and ethnological interest. Associated with them are the Habus and the Dhahuriyin tribes. Together they number about 6,000 persons in Ras al Khaimah, with about another 1,000 working temporarily in the other emirates, mainly in Abu Dhabi. The tribe, however, spreads out into Oman and is largely concentrated in the Musandum Peninsula.

The Shihuh are very independent but do not repudiate allegiance to the Ruler of Ras al Khaimah, on whom they rely for help or protection in any crisis. The tribe is composed of two elements; one is of Arabian and the other of Iranian origin, the latter known as Kumazorah and supposed to be of Baluchi descent. The Arab component probably came from the Yemen many years ago.

The Shihuh are not nomadic, though some of them might be described as being only semi-sedentary in that they have both summer and winter settlements. Geographically the Shihuh area is divided into two zones. The first is a mountain zone where vegetation is very limited and the soil eroded. No wells are found in this zone, and the population is dependent on streams of water which appear after rain and which are guided into cisterns located at suitable points. The cultivated fields are terraced, but their area is very limited in relation to the far greater amount of uncultivable land. The second zone is a coastal strip, where wells can be sunk and *aflaj* have been constructed.

The predominant unit of settlement in the mountain zone is a hamlet occupied by one or more family groups. The settlements in the coastal zone tend to be nucleated, that is, grouped together with the various families temporarily integrated. The only exceptions to this general pattern are a few permanent settlements of fishermen. The crops grown include small quantities of barley and wheat in the mountain zone, and dates in the coastal area. Goat breeding is carried on extensively and provides a surplus for sale in the markets of Ras al Khaimah outside Shihuh territory. Some of the goats are kept in pens and the manure is collected for sale to the farms at Digdagga. The date gardens also provide a surplus for sale, but the cereal crops are seldom sufficient even for the growers' own needs.

The Shihuh have many unusual, indeed odd, customs, some of which have been described earlier in this book. Though strangers are not welcome in Shihuh territory, the traveller, whoever he may be, is to be helped on his way, and Professor Walter Dostal of Berne University tells us that "The traveller who passes through Shihuh territory will find water jars under trees; these jars are supplied with water by the women every day and their purpose is to refresh thirsty travellers. They are donated by richer men in order to increase their local prestige. The donor buys the water jar and pays one of the families living nearby to fill it each day" (*The Geographical Journal*, March 1972). This custom of helping the wayfarer is reminiscent of that in medieval England, where pious benefactors built bridges, often with a chapel, over rivers and streams to help the traveller or pilgrim.

The houses of the Shihuh in the mountains are built of stone, but on the coast they are of the *barasti* type. Some of the families live in caves with the entrance boarded up to provide privacy and protection from wandering animals. Others are reputed to have lived in pits in the ground, but this seems to be a thing of the past.

SPORTS AND PASTIMES

Sports in Trucial Oman tended to be of the robust kind, hunting and hawking being especially favoured. Hawking is a seasonal sport and is confined to the winter and spring months, when the lesser bustard (*habara*) visits the area, feeding on the desert vegetation which springs up after the rains. Nowadays, however, the bustard does not seem to frequent the Gulf area in such large numbers as formerly, and hunting trips may be organized by Gulf devotees of the sport to places as far away as Pakistan.

Hawks are regarded as very personal possessions, and a shaikh may be accompanied by his hawks and their keepers almost everywhere he goes. The birds will be brought into his *majalis*, or reception room, and they will be with him when he entertains in the evening. Each hawk is given a name of its own, which is always used when referring to the bird. Bedouins display great skill in training and handling their hawks. Training is a job for a specialist, but a good hawker can train a bird in a few weeks. This is borne out by Thesiger, who in his book entitled *Arabian Sands* states: "I have been told that in England it takes fifty days to train a wild falcon, but here [Buraimi] the Arabs had them ready in a fortnight to three weeks. This is because they are never separated from them. A man who was training a falcon carried it about everywhere with him. He even fed with it sitting on his left wrist and slept with it perched on its block beside his head. Always he was stroking it, speaking to it, hooding it and unhooding it." Trained hawks are expensive to buy and expensive to keep, as they require a substantial ration of meat each day and unless tended by a specialist may fall ill and die. But though hawking is a sport for shaikhs and rich men, others are able to participate in the hunts, including friends, staff, keepers, and servants. Many of the latter look forward to the hunting season much as in Scotland the gillies used to look forward to the "Twelfth".

A hawk is carried about on the gloved hand or arm of its keeper. Tough leather gloves or an armlet made of carpet material are very necessary to protect the hands or arms from the sharp claws of the bird. The armlet type of glove is very common as it enables the hawk to be transferred easily to the hand and arm of another person. Owners generally like to talk to their hawk and pet it from time to time, and so the hawk is transferred from the keeper on frequent occasions. A cord fastened to the glove or armlet but capable of quick release is attached at its other end to one leg of the hawk. A small leather hood which can easily be removed is kept over the hawk's head until a hunt starts. A good well-trained hawk will when hunting bring down four or five bustards, perhaps more if it has not been fed beforehand. After each kill, the hawk is given a titbit of the prey to eat. A perch shaped like an outsize mushroom or golf-ball tee is provided for the hawk when it is resting or sleeping.

Camel-racing, as well as horse-racing, are much esteemed in the Gulf emirates, and the races attract large crowds though these will be all male. In some Arab countries camel-racing is regarded as a comic interlude between the serious business of horse-racing. The camels are poorly trained; some may decide to set off in the opposite direction to the others and some may even sit down, but this is not so in Trucial Oman: the camels of the area are of especially fine breed and are generally regarded as the best of their kind, fetching higher prices than camels from other regions. In the past, camels were an important export from the area, and they are still sought after by discerning buyers. In Abu Dhabi a camel-race is quite an occasion. As many as forty camels at a time may participate in a race, making two circuits of a long course. The camels show a remarkable turn of speed and the races are eagerly watched by an expert and discerning public. At one such race meeting which the author was privileged to attend, the race-goers were obviously very well informed and keenly interested in the animals. With but some small concessions to modern times, the scene was obviously like those which must have been enacted time and time again in the past. It was indeed a "gathering of the tribes", all wearing their traditional dress and many of them carrying a muzzle-loading gun with a feather in the barrel; this seems to be the correct procedure on such occasions. On one side of the writer there sat a veteran with a very long gun and next to him a sturdy warrior with crossed cartridge bandoliers, a rifle, and a silver-ornamented dagger tucked in his waist-band. On the other side, there was a superb hawk resting on the gloved left arm of his keeper, who from time to time produced a paper bag from which he extracted scraps of red meat to feed to the hawk.

Chapter 15

Archaeology

Civilizations have come and gone. Some have been well documented; some have left magnificent monuments behind them; others have left few traces, and yet others have been completely forgotten. Occasionally some forgotten civilization has come to light; one such is that of the area we now know as the United Arab Emirates and the Sultanate of Oman. Only during the past decade has the archaeologist's spade revealed the existence in Abu Dhabi of a civilization which stretches back into the third millennium BC and which appears to have lasted some 2,000 years. This was not just a hunting or pastoral economy, though finds of arrow-heads suggest that the people were hunters as well as owners of domesticated animals such as sheep, goats, and donkeys, and possibly camels. They were a people having regular settlements, and constructors of substantial stone buildings dating back before the Bronze Age. They obviously had a great respect for the newly dead, for elaborate tombs and sepulchres have been found. These are not like the pyramids of Egypt, designed for a great king or chief, but were communal graves and intended for a succession of burials. But not much regard was paid to those long dead, and their bones were pushed aside to make room for the new. The tombs suggest that the political or tribal outlook was more democratic than authoritarian, and that there was no worship of any king-god. The people appear to have been peaceful rather than warlike, as few weapons have been discovered, nor have hilltop forts been found.

Many intriguing questions arise in connection with this forgotten civilization. Whence did the people come? What happened to them eventually and why were they forgotten? Did they cultivate cereal crops, as is suggested by the finds of a number of querns? If this were so, surely the climate must have been different from what it is now and the rainfall must have been heavier. They must also have lived at a standard considerably beyond that of bare subsistence, or how could they have provided the labour to transport huge stone blocks from the hills and to fashion them into shape, ornamenting them in bas-relief? Were they just fishermen on the coasts and agriculturalists inland? This is more than doubtful, judging from their monuments. The question is: were they traders, carriers, or, may it be suggested, miners and smelters of copper ores found in the mountains of Oman?

Interest in Abu Dhabi's ancient past was first kindled when oil prospectors brought back tales of grave mounds and scraps of pottery which they had found in now desolate areas. The impetus to research was given by Mr Tim Hillyard of the Abu Dhabi Marine Areas Oil Company, himself an amateur archaeologist, who discovered in 1958 burial mounds "somewhat like those of Bahrain" on the island of Um an Nar (The Mother of Fire). This was a small island, difficult of access and scarcely a square mile in area, separated by a narrow stretch of water from the mainland of Abu Dhabi near the Makta Bridge, which joins the larger island of Abu Dhabi Town to its hinterland. Mr Hillyard passed information about the findings to a Danish archaeological expedition then working in Bahrain, where there are literally thousands of somewhat similar burial mounds. This must not however be taken to mean that the cultures are identical, for the grave mound is to be found in many different cultures. Professor P. V. Glob and Dr Geoffrey Bibby from the Pre-history Museum of Aarhus, who were leading the Danish team in Bahrain, made a short visit in 1959 to investigate the finds at Um an Nar, and in the following year they commenced excavations which continued until 1965.

Though it has now become the site of a new oil refinery, Um an Nar was then practically a desert island, with only a single date palm to relieve its bareness. The mounds, which were buried in sand, did not at first sight look very impressive, but on excavation they were found to be the debris of collapsed stone buildings, of which the largest was very elaborate. All the buildings were circular in shape, with their walls sloping slightly inwards and constructed of dry stone, that is, without the use of cement or mortar. The smaller tombs were built of rough quarried stone, but the larger ones were built with chiselled limestone blocks, carefully shaped so as to form a circular wall. In all, there were at least fifty mounds, some quite small and looking like heaps of tumbled stone, with triangular entrances.

Ring walls surround some of the larger tombs, but this is not an unusual feature, as such a wall serves to mark out the perimeter and prevents material from sliding outwards during construction. The ring walls of the larger mounds were exceptionally well built, with cut limestone blocks each a foot high and about three feet long. Their outer faces were shaped as a curve to follow the circular plan of the building. Their edges were neatly cut to fit snugly against each other. The largest tombs were about twelve yards in diameter and the smallest less than two yards across. One building excavated was about thirty feet in diameter and its walls were some six or seven feet high. Originally it had a dome-shaped roof of rock slabs supported inside by several walls which served to provide a number of small rooms each paved with stone slabs. The tombs were intended for a succession of burials, unlike those in Bahrain, which are single tombs for single burials. Some of the tombs in Um an Nar are decorated with reliefs of animals, including oryx, bulls, and a camel. Such stones originally flanked the entrance to the tombs.

All the tombs excavated except the smallest contained human skeletons, some with thirty or forty such skeletons, far more than could have been accommodated had they all been buried at the same time. The grave-gifts which had accompanied them to the tomb included pottery, stone beads, copper pins, and daggers. The pots and vases had been thrown on a potter's wheel; they were well made, thin, and decorated with elaborate geometric designs on red-brown or grey clay. Two of the pots carried friezes depicting humped bulls, and they have been dated by the archaeologists at about the middle of the third millennium BC.

Near the burial mounds but situated on the coast, there was a village of some twenty to thirty stone-built houses, which are surprisingly spacious, the largest over 300 square feet in area and containing seven rooms, each ten feet wide and up to thirty-five feet in length. In these houses pottery was found similar to that of the tombs, and in addition many articles which give some idea of how the people of the settlement lived and worked. There were copper fish-hooks and stone weights of local limestone pierced with a central hole, probably used for sinking fish nets, or less probably as loom weights. Several stone querns were found, which suggest that the inhabitants must have cultivated grain. Lying around were many animal bones including those of sheep, goats, gazelles, and camels. The camel bones were an unexpected find, as previously it had been assumed that the camel was domesticated at a later period than that of the settlement. More numerous, however, than all the other kinds of bones were the bones of the dugong or sea-cow. The dugong is a seal-like mammal about the size of a man which is still occasionally found in the coastal waters of Abu Dhabi. Swimming upright, the dugong could be mistaken at a distance for some form of human being, and this has been said to be the origin of the myth of the mermaid.

Houses in the village were closely grouped in the centre, with the more spacious houses located on the outskirts, but the most surprising and unique feature of the houses is the solidity of their structure. Such substantial, stone-built residences were unknown in the region during later historical periods. Barasti huts constructed from palm leaves were all but universal among fishermen, and indeed still are. Anything more substantial, moreover, is constructed of sun-baked bricks and not of stone. Even the forts erected in the 18th and 19th centuries were built of mud. They need periodical repair after any heavy fall of rain, and the commander of a troop of the Trucial Oman Scouts quartered in one such fort in Al Ain is reported to have told the correspondent of Newsweek (28 March 1966): "We could stand up indefinitely to bullets, but God help us if they ever started using water pistols."

Um an Nar must surely have been something more than a small fishing village. Perhaps it was a trading terminal or a small port, for how could a few poor fishermen provide themselves with such excellent housing? It would seem also that the climate must then have been different from what it is today, and this point is made by Dr Bibby in his book entitled Looking for Dilmun (Collins, 1970, page 306): "The community we were excavating was one which was geared to a different climate, in particular to a greater rainfall, than that of the present day."

In 1959, Shaikh Zaid, then Governor of the Eastern Province, invited Professor Glob and Dr Bibby to visit the Al Ain Oasis so that he could show them some burial mounds in the Hafit area, which appeared to be like those of Um an Nar.

During the next few years, several of these mounds were investigated; from a bronze sword found in one of the tombs the mounds were dated to the late second millennium BC. Further investigation disclosed that the Hafit mounds contained burials from two periods: the Jamdat Nasr Period, about 3000 BC; and the late second millennium BC or early first millennium BC. Some are perhaps even more recent.

During the winter of 1964–65 a stone tomb was excavated at Hili, and in 1968 a Danish team under the leadership of Miss Karen Frifelt began work on the site. Since then the work of excavation has continued during the winter and spring months of each year. This team discovered a settlement where the tomb had already been excavated. The first tombs to be examined there proved to be of an ordinary type, consisting of rocks heaped up around a central chamber. The evidence collected from pottery shards, bronze vessels, and a bronze sword showed that they were at least 1,000 years later than the Um an Nar settlement. Further excavation, however, yielded an impressive monument of the Um an Nar type but bigger and built up with large sandstone blocks. Some of these stones, which had functioned as door-posts, carried relief carvings of human beings and animals. These decorations are lively in design and of some artistic merit. One of the reliefs shows a man riding a donkey followed by a second man on foot. Another carving depicts two cheetahs or lions devouring a gazelle. Yet another bas-relief is of a pair of lovers, and there is also an impressionistic carving of a long-horned animal.

Pottery shards were found in great abundance, from vessels predominantly similar to those found in Um an Nar but more varied. The pottery finds proved that the monument belonged to the same cultural pattern revealed at Um an Nar, and this is pretty conclusive evidence that the two sites belonged to the same period and the same people. Pottery, here as always, proved to be the archaeologist's best friend for classifying and dating these early civilizations. A pottery vessel is so fragile that if dropped it breaks into many pieces, yet the pieces are most enduring, able to survive through the millennia, neither rusting like metal, rotting like timber, nor decomposing like textiles.

Though of the same period, the remains at Hili are far more imposing than those at Um an Nar, and the size and weight of the stone blocks suggest that this was a settlement of some stability over a long period of years; and with a sufficient surplus labour force above the needs of agriculture to allow for the quarrying, shaping, and decorating of the huge stone slabs, and the transporting of them from the mountains several miles away. The site is not that of some commanding hilltop but a plain now somewhat arid and some distance from the nearest cultivated fields. The settlement so far excavated is a fortified tower protected by a moat, but it is not difficult to imagine that, in its time, the site was surrounded by cultivated lands yielding ample supplies of vegetables, fruit, and probably cereals. The environmental change has no doubt been brought about by the depredation of uncontrolled grazing by goats and other animals, by soil erosion, by human neglect, and by a more than probable change in climate.

The Hili settlement is not an isolated village, as there are several other settlements within some twenty miles. In one area between Al Ain village and the Jebel Hafit (*jebel* means hill or mountain) there are hundreds of burial mounds, now covered with sand and situated at the foot of the hills or on their slopes or on top of ridges. The tombs, as elsewhere in.Abu Dhabi, are communal and are circular in shape, with an entrance and a passageway on the south side. They are built from unshaped or roughly cut stone. Nearly all have been entered at later times through a hole in the top, for new burials at a much later date, or by grave-robbers. The oldest burials, at the bottom of the mounds, can be dated from their pottery to what is known as the Jamdat Nasr period. Apart from pottery the graves have yielded small beads of clay, cornelian, and bone, and a few copper nails and pins. One tomb contained a beehive-shaped steatite jar and painted red pottery related to the Um an Nar and Hili finds. The later burials in the mounds were accompanied by iron fragments, and must therefore be dated at least 2,000 years later than the first burials.

At yet another site, named Bint Sa'ud, stone graves from at least three different periods were found at the foot of, and at the top of, a rocky eminence. Some Jamdat Nasr graves from about 3000 BC were discovered, but they had been plundered by grave-robbers and on top of some of them later tombs had been built. One of the graves, though it had been robbed and partly destroyed, retained enough of the original structure for its outlines to be traced and to show that it was similar to the tombs of Um an Nar.

This rectangular stone tomb, with two chambers and a connecting passage, was found to contain several burials. The area around the structure, covered by stones from fallen walls, had been used for many burials which appear to have been later than the original burials in the two chambers, and may be dated to the 8th century BC. It is possible also that some of the intruding burials in the chambers may have been from this more recent period. The scene presented by the remains is very confused and it is not easy to discover and define the sequence of burials.

The tombs yielded an unusually rich harvest of grave-goods, including four bronze daggers, two bronze bowls, a bronze axe-head, about a hundred bronze arrow-heads, one bronze spear-head with its socket, one complete steatite jar complete with its lid, and several beads of cornelian, bone, and shell, besides pottery shards, and fragments of a great number of steatite vessels and their lids.

The bronze finds suggest a date of about 1000 BC but the original structure was much older, as the later tomb had been built on top of the older one.

In the emirates other than Abu Dhabi, practically no archaeological research has been undertaken, and these areas remain virgin ground for the excavators of the future. Possible sites which might repay investigation are Ras al Khaimah and Dibba. Ras al Khaimah may possibly have been a sea-port in ancient times, and several miles north of Ras al Khaimah Town there are numerous burial mounds, while at Dibba on the Batinah Coast, pottery, steatite vessels, and arrow-heads have been found which appear to belong to the same culture as late Bint Sa'ud and the secondary burials in the Hafit mountain. It is to be hoped that the archaeologists will continue their work in the Sultanate of Oman, so that some link may be found with what we know about the ancient civilization of Abu Dhabi. It would be especially interesting if more could be discovered about the mining and presumably the smelting of copper ore in the area.

LATER ARCHAEOLOGICAL MONUMENTS

There is an immense gap between what we know of the prehistoric peoples of the region and the later still surviving archaeological monuments in the form of forts, watch-towers, *aflaj*, or wind-towers. What became of the prehistoric peoples we do not know, but the world seems to have passed the region by, and they disappeared, probably because of the decay of the great civilizations of Mesopotamia, of the Indus, and of Persia. The monuments we have now to consider are to be dated well within historical times, most of them going no further back than the 18th or early 19th centuries.

Mention has already been made of the *aflaj*, so we do not need to consider these again except to remark that their beginnings appear to go back many centuries and that they were probably first built by skilled immigrant workers from Iran.

Castles and forts are to be found scattered up and down the region. Several are located in the Al Ain region, and one of them now houses an excellent museum which provides the best available visual evidence of the culture of prehistoric times through its display of the finds from Um an Nar, Hili, and the other sites. In the Liwa Oasis there are also several forts and watch towers, but many of them are now rather dilapidated. In Abu Dhabi Town the old fort or castle is still in the author's opinion the building with most character. It was originally built in 1793 but has been renovated several times. The old guard-tower by the Makta bridge dates back, as do so many others in the Federation, to the early 19th century. Interesting palaces or forts are to be seen in Ajman and Um al Quaiwain, but they have now become less romantic-looking as a result of the building of modern houses around them.

Particularly interesting buildings are the old wind-towers, still to be seen in their original state in Sharjah and Dubai. They were also to be found in Abu Dhabi, but unfortunately the last there was demolished a year or two ago to make room for new buildings.

These wind-towers were a feature of many of the older houses, and in Sharjah are some especially fine specimens which it is greatly hoped will be preserved. In Dubai also many are still standing, and a preservation order has been made so that at least a few will be preserved as historical monuments to remind coming generations of the skills and technical achievements of their forebears. The wind-tower is a tall rectangular tower somewhat like an Italian campanile, with openings on each side so as to catch any breeze which may blow, whatever its direction. Connected with the rooms below, the towers act much like a fan in providing air movement, thus making life much more comfortable for the occupants during the hot summer weather. Locally the towers are known as *badkeer*, which is a Persian word meaning "wind-intake". At one time wind-towers were common in most of the Gulf states. Bahrain still has many fine examples, but in Kuwait all disappeared some years ago in the rush towards modernization.

Summary and Conclusion

Throughout the United Arab Emirates the winds of change are blowing strongly, and development has proceeded at an astonishingly rapid pace though it is only about fifteen years since the first crude oil was exported in 1962. Now these exports have exceeded 50 million tons and show every prospect of further expansion as new oilfields come into production not only in Abu Dhabi but also in Dubai and Sharjah. Oil export in the Federation can be likened to an electric power-station providing the energy to run the economy, while the concurrent development of transport and communications can be likened to a distributive network through which the energy, in the form of wealth from oil, is spread over the economy. Two great international airports are in full operation, while a third, though smaller, ranks high in operational efficiency. Two large modern sea-ports have been constructed and a number of smaller ports have been revived and improved. Especially important has been the construction of a network of trunk roads which is now being further extended. These new roads are opening up the entire area so that formerly remote parts are being put into easy, rapid, and cheap contact with each other and with the capital towns. Another factor of great importance has been the development of supplies of electrical energy. Now all the capital towns and an increasing number of the smaller towns have electricity available to them. Apart from the obvious advantages of cheap electricity for lighting and domestic use and for the smaller industries, it is in effect helping to conquer the harsh climate through air conditioning. Formerly, without adequate surfaced roads, without sufficient supplies of sweet water, without electric lighting and without air conditioning, life was hardly tolerable in the hot, humid months of high summer.

All in all the transformation which has taken place over the past ten years, and more especially during the past five years, is truly astonishing and it would not be exaggerating to claim that the rapidity and extent of this development is unrivalled in any other part of the world. Some of the most modern and sophisticated applications of technology are being pioneered in the emirates, such as the controlled-environment agricultural project on Sadiyat Island or the submerged water–oil displacement storage tanks serving Dubai's oilfield. Now being constructed in Dubai is the world's largest dry dock for tankers.

Schools, hospitals, clinics, and modern houses have been built in all the emirates, and in the larger towns modern apartment-blocks, offices, banks, and supermarkets are springing up at an astonishing rate, so that what were not so long ago small fishing villages or antiquated ports are taking on the appearance of ultra-modern cities.

Material developments, however, are only part of the picture, and it is the less tangible developments in education, training, health services, cultural activities, and social welfare that augur best for the future. Education, as stated earlier, has assumed a high priority, as it has come to be realized in all the emirates that their future progress depends largely on the rate at which nationals become qualified to assume responsibilities in administration, government, medicine, teaching, engineering, and industry. In the past, to achieve their remarkably rapid progress, governments and private enterprise in the emirates have drawn on practically the whole world for high expertise, administrative abilities, specialist skills, and the supporting manual and skilled labour. Now the need is for the nationals of the emirates to shoulder these responsibilities themselves.

For the immediate future the prospects of further development are most favourable and with rapidly mounting oil revenues one may reasonably expect further rapid progress, and indeed over the next three or four years there is likely to be a real boom in constructional and building activities. Thereafter as the infrastructure is largely completed, the construction phase will give place to one of consolidation and the maintenance and improvement of existing facilities. Concurrently there is likely to be a phase in which new industries will be set up, based on oil and natural gas, or serving new needs such as those of the building industry. As standards of living will undoubtedly rise, it may be expected that there will be considerable expansion in what are known as tertiary industries, mainly in the service category, including cultural activities, entertainment, recreation, financial institutions, and improved retail distribution outside the main towns. As for the more distant future it is unwise to speculate, but granted peace and political stability there is some reason to suppose that wise husbanding of resources, foreign investment, and the introduction of new technologies should enable the emirates to maintain a sufficient degree of prosperity.

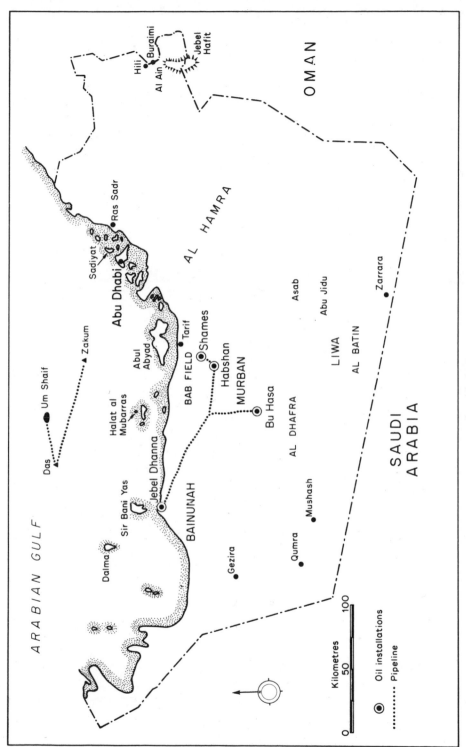

1 Abu Dhabi Emirate

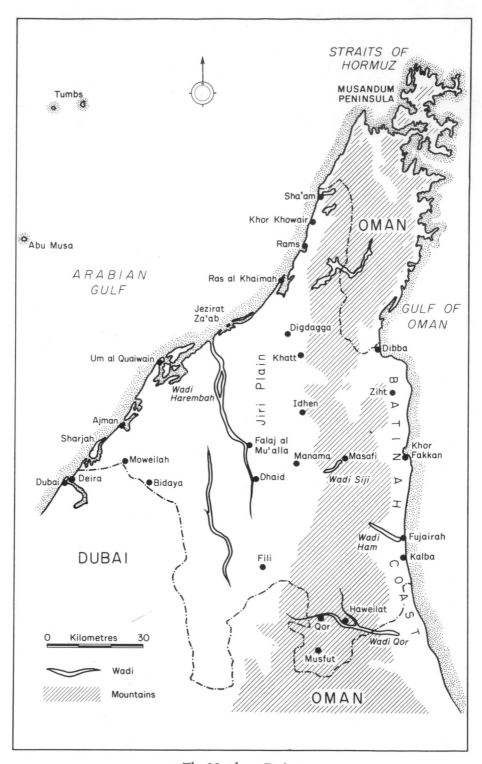

2 The Northern Emirates

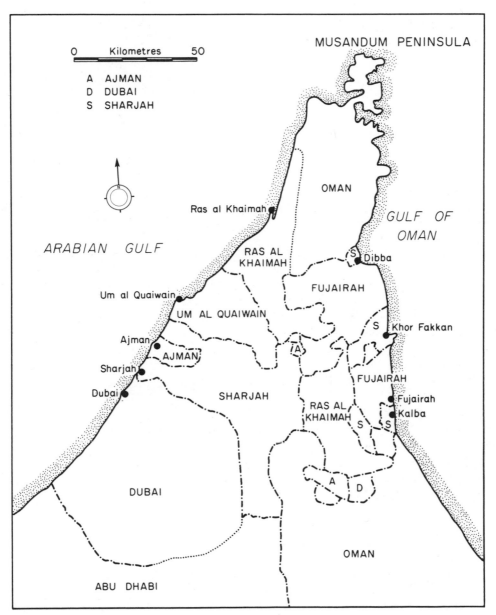

3 The Northern Emirates: Approximate Boundaries

Appendices

Appendix A
Rulers of the United Arab Emirates

		from
Abu Dhabi	Shaikh Zaid bin Sultan al Nahayan	1966
	President of the United Arab Emirates	
Dubai	Shaikh Rashid bin Sa'id al Maktum	1958
	Vice-President of the United Arab Emirates	
Sharjah	Shaikh Sultan bin Mohammed al Qassimi	1972
Ras al Khaimah	Shaikh Saqr bin Mohammed al Qassimi	1948
Ajman	Shaikh Rashid bin Humaid al Naimi	1928
Um al Quaiwain	Shaikh Ahmad bin Rashid al Mualla	1929
Fujairah	Shaikh Hamed bin Mohammed al Sharqi	1974

Appendix B

Appendix B
Statistical Tables

Table 1   United Arab Emirates. Area and Population. 1968 and 1975 Censuses

	Area sq. miles	Population males	females	Total 1968	Total 1975
Abu Dhabi	26,000	34,863	11,512	46,375	235,662
Dubai	1,500	35,620	23,351	58,971	206,861
Sharjah	1,000	17,660	14,008	31,668	88,188
Ras al Khaimah	650	13,249	11,138	24,387	57,282
Ajman	100	2,212	2,034	4,246	21,566
Um al Quaiwain	300	1,982	1,762	3,744	16,879
Fujairah	450	5,220	4,515	9,735	26,498
Trucial Oman Scouts	—	1,100	—	1,100	—
Totals	30,000	111,906	68,320	180,226	655,937*

Note: The population of the Federation has increased considerably since 1968, especially in
    Abu Dhabi, and is now about 400,000.

* Includes 3,001 persons not classified.

Table 2   United Arab Emirates. Statistical Estimates

Population (1976)	*Males* 400,000
	Females 260,000
	Total 660,000
Houses (1975)	66,000
Oil production (1974)	88 million long tons
Electricity production (1974)	800 million KWH
Liquefied (LNG & LPG) natural gas production (1976)	3 million tons
Economically active population (1975)	175,000
Cultivated area	450 square miles (1,200 square kilometres)
Desert pasture (coarse)	5,000 square miles (13,000 square kilometres)
Imports (1974)	8 billion Dirhams
Motor vehicles (1975)	75,000
National income (1975)	*Total* $7 billion
	Per caput $17,000

Note: The above data are subject to varying margins of error as statistical information relating
    to the UAE is as yet very incomplete.

Table 3   Abu Dhabi Emirate. Economic and Social Indicators. 1967–1974

Year	Crude Oil Pro- duction (million long tons)	Government Revenue (million DH)	Government Expenditure (million DH)			Government International Contributions (million DH)
			Current	Development	Total	
1967	18	410	160	170	330	120
1968	24	550	290	300	590	130
1969	28	680	360	460	820	40
1970	33	860	390	330	720	40
1971	44	1,650	710	390	1,100	260
1972	50	2,180	1,270	460	1,740	310*
1973	62	4,210	2,590	560	3,391	1,220
1974	67	14,271			7,898	n.a.

* includes DH 240 million in capital budget

Year	Cost of Living Index‡ (Sept. 1966 = 100)	Bank Assets end year (million DH)	Number of Motor Vehicles Licensed	Number of Telephone Lines in Use	Foreign Cables In and Out (thousands)	Number of Building Approvals
1967	115	670	n.a.	500	115	n.a.
1968	118	880	n.a.	900	129	582
1969	129	900	7,805	1,200	172	430
1970	137	620	10,187	1,900	157	251
1971	135	900	12,160	2,800	146	509
1972	143§	1,410	17,096	3,810	155	328
1973	165	1,890	25,564	5,201	199	n.a.
1974	215	n.a.	35,593	6,841	218	n.a.

‡ Month of September   § November 1972
n.a. = not available

Table 3 (*continued*)

Year	Imports (million DH)	Cargo Arriving (thousand tons)			Air Freight Arriving (metric tons)	Pupils attending School	Hospital Beds	Estimated Population mid-year* (thousands)
		Ocean Ships	Local Craft	Motor Lorries				
1967	147	144	n.a.	n.a.	n.a.	2,223	50	35
1968	311	244	n.a.	n.a.	n.a.	4,908	132	46
1969	593	272	121	60	2,402	6,972	145	60
1970	352	136	84	56	2,247	9,011	161	75
1971	469	196	97	44	2,591	10,753	256	85
1972	758	377	74	95	3,419	13,925	431	100
1973	1,019	n.a.	n.a.	n.a.	4,711	15,806	472	150
1974	2,200†	582	n.a.	n.a.	7,199	19,002‡	564	200

Notes: * Estimates are unofficial except for 1968 (census year)   *n.a.* = not available
  † Partly estimated
  ‡ In addition 1,258 pupils attended private schools in 1972 and 2,479 in 1974

Table 4   Dubai Emirate. Economic and Social Indicators. 1967–1974

Year	Imports (DH million)	Imports (thousand tons)	Crude Oil Production (million long tons)	Government Revenue* (DH million)	Government Expenditure (DH million)	Number of Motor Vehicles Licensed	Electricity Generated (mill. units)
1967	477	318	—	n.a.	17	n.a.	24
1968	761	468	—	n.a.	21	5,037	42
1969	922	636	0·5	60	60	7,598	69
1970	960	651	4·3	120	85	7,522	98
1971	1,059	742	6·1	150	100	8,601	122
1972	1,476	1,263	7·6	200	140	10,753	179
1973	2,341	1,846	11·0	300	250	14,000	238
1974	4,817	2,963	12·1	350	n.a.	20,000	310

* Estimated

Table 4 (*continued*)

Year	Air Passengers (thousand)			Air Freight (metric tons)		Air Mail (metric tons)		Water produced (million gallons)	Telephone Lines Installed
	In	Out	Transit	In	Out	In	Out		
1967	31	32	18	992	849	48	17	292	1,796
1968	52	52	31	2,469	2,822	61	29	351	2,361
1969	70	69	37	2,706	1,700	65	35	608	2,400
1970	84	84	74	2,906	1,901	79	30	894	3,742
1971	96	93	94	4,148	1,899	85	36	922	5,202
1972	131	131	165	5,178	1,708	n.a.	n.a.	1,014	6,900
1973	165	152	221	5,333	2,096	n.a.	n.a.	1,998	8,511
1974	243	213	283	8,077	3,537	n.a.	n.a.	2,571	10,758

Year	Cables Out (thousands)	International Telecommunications Outwards (thou. paid minutes)		Banks Operating	Bank Assets (DH million)	Hospital Beds	Estimated Population (thousands)
		Telex	Telephone				
1967	61	13	57	8	353	156	59
1968	84	54	91	10	592	156	59
1969	92	74	160	12	929	164	75
1970	92	99	314	14	1,282	204	75
1971	93	163	506	14	1,677	357	75
1972	98	237	944	14	1,975	435	80
1973	119	368	1,217	19	n.a.	500	100
1974	149	671	1,499	30	n.a.	n.a.	150

Table 5   Average Maximum and Minimum Temperatures and Relative Humidities. Abu Dhabi Town.

Year	Month	Temperature Centigrade		Relative Humidity Per cent	
		Av. Max.	*Av. Min.*	*Av. Max*	*Av. Min.*
1971	January	24	13	90	52
	August	39	28	89	46
1972	January	24	14	87	51
	August	42	28	85	27
1973	January	22	12	85	48
	August	42	30	87	32
1974	January	24	14	92	49
	August	40	29	82	37
1975	January	24	15	86	31
	August	40	30	84	40

Measured at the International Airport, Abu Dhabi.

Note: To convert Centigrade to Fahrenheit multiply by 9, divide by 5 and add 32.

Table 6   Rainfall in Abu Dhabi Town.
   Rain years October to September in millimetres and inches

Rain Year	Millimetres	Inches
1966–67	24·5	0·9
1967–68	92·2	3·6
1968–69	58·3	2·3
1969–70	3·2	0·1
1970–71	15·1	0·6
1971–72	62·5	2·5
1972–73	37·8	1·5
1973–74	11·6	0·4
1974–75	80·5	3·1

Rain seldom falls in Abu Dhabi Town between May and October.

Note: Rainfall measured in centre of town up to 1969–1970 and at the airport from 1970-1971 onwards.

Table 7   Abu Dhabi Emirate. Crude Oil Production. 1962–1974
             (Thousand long tons)

Year	ADPC	ADMA	Total
1962	—	785	785
1963	84	2,304	2,388
1964	6,018	2,934	8,952
1965	9,011	4,333	13,344
1966	12,054	4,986	17,040
1967	12,166	5,866	18,032
1968	14,918	8,711	23,629
1969	16,815	11,505	28,320
1970	20,080	12,686	32,766
1971	27,160	16,933	44,093
1972	28,834	20,827	49,661
1973	37,564	23,939	61,728*
1974	43,310	21,816	66,677†

Notes: * Includes 225 thousand long tons produced by ADOC.
         † Includes 661 thousand long tons produced by ADOC and 890 thousand long tons produced by Total-Abu al-Bakhaosh.

Table 8   Abu Dhabi Emirate. Crude Oil Exports. 1962–1974
             (Thousand long tons)

Year	On-shore ADPC	Off-shore ADMA	Total
1962	—	711	711
1963	70	2,295	2,365
1964	5,849	2,929	8,778
1965	8,928	4,312	13,240
1966	12,135	5,062	17,197
1967	12,158	5,702	17,860
1968	14,758	8,738	23,496
1969	16,781	11,543	28,324
1970	20,156	12,649	32,805
1971	26,947	16,833	43,780
1972	28,951	20,715	49,666
1973	37,005	23,943	61,136*
1974	43,172	21,611	66,230†

Notes: * Includes 188 thousand long tons exported by ADOC.
         † Includes 594 thousand long tons exported by ADOC and 853 thousand long tons by Total-Abu al-Bakhaosh.

Table 9   Abu Dhabi Emirate. Tankers Loaded. 1962–1974

Year	ADPC	ADMA	Total
1962	—	22	22
1963	2	67	69
1964	168	81	249
1965	256	110	366
1966	276	135	411
1967	257	175	432
1968	302	217	519
1969	344	219	563
1970	395	254	649
1971	478	226	704
1972	462	262	724
1973	543	287	835*
1974	627	283	937†

Notes: * Includes 5 tankers loaded by ADOC.
† Includes 12 tankers loaded by ADOC and 15 by Total-Abu al-Bakhaosh.

Table 10   Abu Dhabi. Main Destinations of Crude Oil Exports. 1974 (Million long tons)

Country	Long tons Million
Japan	24
France	14
UK	6
USA	5
West Germany	4
Switzerland	2
Netherlands	2
Canada	1
Sweden	1
Other countries	7
Total	66

Table 11   Abu Dhabi. Crude Oil Exports by Companies. 1974

Company	Million long tons	Tankers loaded number
ADPC	43·1	627
ADMA	21·6	283
ADOC	0·6	12
Total-Abu al- Bakhaosh	0·9	15
Total	66·2	937

Table 12a   Dubai Emirate. Imports by Main Commodity Groups. 1968–1972 (million DH)

Commodity Group	1968	1969	1970	1971	1972	1973
Household goods	179	202	179	208	274	346
Foodstuffs	118	114	132	150	199	283
Textiles and clothing	148	164	145	134	215	389
Machinery	151	187	156	192	250	400
Building materials	74	101	139	142	153	326
Electrical, radio, and allied goods	31	44	63	55	67	98
Stationery	5	7	6	7	11	17
Photographic goods	2	4	6	4	8	10
Cosmetics	7	8	9	9	13	21
Medicines and chemicals	9	9	9	19	16	31
Fuel and oil	12	28	27	27	84	121
Arms and ammunition	1	6	18	10	5	10
Oilfield materials	26	45	64	90	165	273
Liquor and wines	3	4	6	11	15	17
Totals	761	922	960	1,059	1,475	2,341

Note: Columns may not add to totals because of rounding.

In 1974 the classification of imports was changed to bring it more into line with the standard International Trade Classification (SITC)

Table 12b   Dubai Emirate. Imports by Main Commodity Groups. 1974

Commodity group	Million Dirhams	Thousand tons
Food and live animals	662	282
Beverages and tobacco	88	15
Crude materials, inedible (except fuels)	102	119
Mineral fuels, lubricants and related materials	435	1,131
Animal and vegetable oils and fats	31	12
Chemicals	153	41
Manufactured goods classified chiefly by material	1,328	1,074
Miscellaneous manufactured articles	538	28
Machinery and transport equipment	1,037	100
Oilfield materials	412	159
Unclassified	30	2
Totals	4,817	2,963

Table 13   Dubai Emirate. Imports by Main Countries of Provenance. 1969–1974
(million DH)

Country	1969	1970	1971	1972	1973	1974
United Kingdom	161	197	186	191	281	577
Japan	179	163	182	308	529	942
United States	76	88	127	200	329	580
Switzerland	106	83	94	110	104	136
India	42	56	47	54	78	182
West Germany	39	32	36	43	86	219
Hong Kong	29	32	36	58	99	140
China	33	30	34	47	81	168
Holland	20	26	32	42	42	98
Pakistan	35	21	25	29	52	125
Saudi Arabia	23	23	23	77	16	36
Italy	17	21	21	22	43	92
Iran	9	14	20	14	82	260
Australia	14	17	18	22	44	75
France	17	14	16	33	70	125
Singapore	15	15	15	19	40	73
Bahrain	6	7	12	11	28	58
Denmark	6	8	10	11	18	34
Lebanon	8	9	10	23	19	17
Other Countries	87	109	115	161	300	880
Totals	922	965	1,059	1,475	2,341	4,817

Table 14   Abu Dhabi Emirate. Imports by Main Commodity Groups. 1969–1971 (Commodities of which imports exceeded 5 million Dirhams in any one of the years.)

Commodity	Million Dirhams		
	1969	*1970*	*1971*
Machinery	143	76	55
Motor vehicles	64	35	42
Building materials	22	21	23
Foodstuffs	43	37	49
Spare parts	41	25	33
Pipes and pipe fittings	33	10	12
Electrical goods	25	20	20
Cement	21	5	6
Household furniture	21	6	6
Motor oil and grease	19	15	15
Tools and hardware	15	11	12
Steel bars and items	14	10	11
Air conditioners	14	5	7
Cables	12	6	7
Textiles	9	9	12
Household appliances	8	5	6
Cigarettes and tobacco	6	6	9
Medicines	6	6	6
Alcoholic drinks	5	3	5
Tyres and tubes	5	4	5
Oilfield equipment	1	11	85
Arms and ammunition	4	2	8
Other commodities	62	25	35
Total	593	353	469

Note: In 1972 the classification of commodities was modified to bring it into line with the International Classification known as SITC.

Table 15 Abu Dhabi Emirate. Imports by Commodity Groups. 1972–1973 (million Dirhams)

Commodity Group	1972	1973
Food and live animals	69	75
Beverages	6	8
Tobacco	7	9
Crude materials, inedible except fuels	8	16
Mineral fuels, lubricants and related materials	27	36
Animal and vegetable oils and fats	4	3
Chemicals	26	31
Manufactured goods classified mainly by material	182	214
Machinery	279	402
Transport equipment	84	155
Miscellaneous manufactured articles	50	65
Other commodities	15	5
Total	757	1,019

Table 16   Abu Dhabi Emirate. Imports by Main Countries of Provenance. 1971–1974 (million Dirhams)

Country	1971	1972	1973	1974
United Kingdom	145	181	280	515
United States	107	104	203	340
Dubai	43	58*	—	—
Japan	26	118	124	336
Holland	16	21	29	56
West Germany	21	44	72	243
Italy	12	20	20	70
Australia	11	14	26	40
France	10	56	64	94
Lebanon	10	22	25	127
Iran	8	7	6	22
Pakistan	6	11	11	32
Saudi Arabia	5	9	10	23
Denmark	6	9	7	18
India	5	12	16	36
Belgium	5	7	22	31
Bahrain	5	10	21	48
Sweden	3	7	6	17
Switzerland	3	10	5	13
Other Countries	22	38	72	205
Totals	469	758	1,019	2,266

* January to September only. Thereafter trade with Dubai became federal, not international.

Table 17   Abu Dhabi and Dubai Emirates. Import Breakdown. 1969–1973

Year	ABU DHABI Million Dirhams				
	1969	1970	1971	1972	1973
Capital goods & construction materials	417	229	306	524	756
Consumer goods other than durables	87	80	100	135	161
Consumer durables	89	44	63	98	102
Totals	593	353	469	757	1,019

Table 17 (*continued*)

Year	DUBAI *Million Dirhams*				
	1969	1970	1971	1972	1973
Capital goods & construction materials	365	391	444	642	1,029
Consumer goods other than durables	356	359	402	647	909
Consumer durables★	201	210	213	245	403
Totals	922	960	1,059	1,534	2,341

★ Includes watches.

	ABU DHABI *Per cent of total*				
	1969	1970	1971	1972	1973
Capital goods & construction materials	70·3	64·9	65·3	69·0	74·1
Consumer goods other than durables	14·7	22·7	21·3	18·0	15·9
Consumer durables	15·0	12·4	13·4	13·0	10·0
Total	100·0	100·0	100·0	100·0	100·0

	DUBAI *Per cent of total*				
	1969	1970	1971	1972	1973
Capital goods & construction materials	39·6	40·7	41·9	43·6	44·0
Consumer goods other than durables	38·6	37·4	38·0	39·4	38·8
Consumer durables	21·8	21·9	20·1	17·0	17·2
Total	100·0	100·0	100·0	100·0	100·0

Table 18   Abu Dhabi. Electricity Production.

Year	Installed Capacity Thousand KW	Maximum Load Thousand KW	Electric Energy Produced Million KWH
1966	3·25	1	8
1967	7·65	3	25
1968	12·00	7·5	60
1969	25·80	14·9	100
1970	81·00	27·9	140
1971	81·00	38·8	210
1972	99·50	53·4	255
1973	114·50	79·9	382
1974	150·50	104·0	454*

*Partly estimated.

Table 19   Abu Dhabi. Water Consumption.

Year	Million gallons per day
1968	2·0
1969	2·0
1970	3·8
1971	4·4
1972	5·1
1973	6·0
1974	6·6

Table 20   Abu Dhabi Emirate. Retail Shops. Autumn 1972

Category	Shops	Workers	Average workers per shop
Grocers	487	877	1·8
Fruit and vegetables	143	262	1·8
Butchers	40	106	2·7
Bakers	34	174	5·1
Fishmongers	16	49	3·1
Clothing, textiles, and footwear	239	650	2·7
Household goods	38	102	2·7
Furniture	36	162	4·5
Electrical goods (including radio)	80	406	5·1
Pharmacists	14	51	3·6
Books and stationery	8	19	2·4
Motor vehicles and spares	68	322	4·7
Machinery and spares	18	125	7·0
Building materials	50	257	5·1
Jewellery	37	96	2·6
General shops and supermarkets	58	433	7·5
Other shops	96	259	2·7
Totals	1,462	4,350	3·0

Note: Many shops stock a variety of goods. These have been classified according to the main commodity sold. Where the variety is very large and no item preponderates, they have been classified as general shops. This category includes the supermarkets.

Table 21   Abu Dhabi Emirate. Service Industries. Autumn 1972

Service	Establishments	Workers	Average workers per establishment
Coffee shops, restaurants, etc.	219	940	4·3
Tailors	160	572	3·6
Laundries	79	432	5·5
Barbers and hairdressers	99	180	1·8
Photographic studios	39	104	2·7
Travel agents	11	90	8·2
Petrol filling stations	34	160	4·7

Table 22   Abu Dhabi Emirate. Manufacturing and Repair Industries. Autumn 1972

Industry	Workshops	Workers	Average workers per workshop
Motor vehicle repair and maintenance	170	930	5·5
Carpentry and woodworking	27	285	10·6
Metal working	12	166	13·3
Air-conditioner repair	28	93	3·3

Table 23   Dubai and Abu Dhabi International Airports. Air Traffic. 1967–1974

Year	Thousand Passengers			Freight (metric tons)	
	Arriving	Departing	Transit	Incoming	Outgoing
			DUBAI		
1967	31	32	18	992	849
1968	52	52	31	2,469	2,822
1969	70	69	37	2,706	1,700
1970	84	84	74	2,906	1,901
1971	96	93	94	4,148	1,859
1972	131	131	165	5,178	1,708
1973	165	152	221	5,333	2,096
1974	243	213	283	8,077	3,537
			ABU DHABI		
1968	27	23	n.a.	n.a.	n.a.
1969	47	44	24	2,402	367
1970	50	50	47	2,247	574
1971	59	57	54	2,591	876
1972	82	81	61	3,419	863
1973	101	100	84	4,711	1,179
1974	164	153	138	7,199	3,922

Table 24 Abu Dhabi Emirate. Cargoes brought into Abu Dhabi. Tonnage Off-loaded and Number of Craft or Vehicles. 1971

Month	Ocean-going Vessels		Local Craft Tugs & Barges		Aircraft		Road Vehicles		Total Cargo
	No.	Tons	No.	Tons	No.	Tons	No.	Tons	Tons
Jan.	20	12,921	60	5,400	234	195	978	5,379	23,895
Feb.	12	11,194	117	11,115	194	178	1,487	8,922	31,409
March	18	7,346	75	7,125	214	219	1,138	6,828	21,518
April	19	9,234	59	5,664	216	178	342	2,565	17,641
May	17	10,368	102	9,103	242	189	598	3,289	22,949
June	25	37,711	76	6,075	228	200	366	2,013	45,999
July	12	8,422	135	9,745	245	204	231	1,346	19,717
August	25	27,729	116	9,874	256	212	382	2,230	40,045
Sept.	22	19,441	100	8,750	240	188	301	1,470	29,849
Oct.	25	19,447	104	9,022	266	348	502	2,598	31,415
Nov.	20	10,216	83	7,885	242	286	680	3,400	21,787
Dec.	21	24,012	75	7,185	242	194	757	4,245	35,636
Totals	236	198,041*	1,102	96,943	2,819	2,591	7,762	44,285	341,860

* Deadweight tons. In freight tons equivalent 265,786 tons. A freight ton is 40 cubic feet for merchandise or 42 cubic feet for timber.

Table 25 United Arab Emirates. Pupils attending Government Schools (at start of school year)

	1968–69	*1969–70*	*1970–71*	*1971–72*	*1972–73*	*1973–74*
Kindergarten	578	788	1,114	76	3,276	2,135
Primary	14,790	18,373	22,009	26,130	30,495	34,731
Preparatory & secondary	1,941	2,510	3,199	4,385	4,668	5,786
Teacher training	189	156	156	156	117	175
Islamic studies	—	—	809	809	1,216	1,192
Vocational	367	498	458	555	421	313
Total	17,865	22,325	27,745	32,111	40,193	44,332

Note: During 1973–1974 there were in addition about 4,000 pupils attending private schools.

Table 26   Abu Dhabi Emirate. Pupils attending Government Schools.
(At start of school year)

School Year	Boys	Girls	Infants	Total
1960–61	81	—	—	81
1961–62	109	—	—	109
1962–63	281	—	—	281
1963–64	340	131	—	471
1964–65	349	138	—	487
1965–66	390	138	—	528
1966–67	579	223	—	802
1967–68	1,499	724	—	2,223
1968–69	2,936	1,394	578	4,908
1969–70	4,104	2,080	788	6,972
1970–71	5,304	2,593	1,114	9,011
1971–72	7,125	3,552	76*	10,753
1972–73	8,379	4,400	1,137	13,916†
1973–74	9,043	5,398	1,365	15,806‡
1974–75	9,882	6,643	2,477	19,002

Notes: * As a temporary measure, some kindergarten classes were suspended to accommodate pupils of other grades.

† In addition to this total, 1,258 pupils were attending private schools, and 2,603 persons were enrolled in "anti-illiteracy" and adult-education classes.

‡ In 1974–5 there were some 2,500 pupils attending private schools and 2,550 attending adult classes. In addition there were 2,894 adult students in the Police and Defence Force schools or in the Labour Camp School on Das Island.

Table 27 Abu Dhabi. Age Distribution of Pupils in Government Schools.

Age	1974/1975		
	Boys	Girls	Total
Under 6	36	47	83
6	1,001	874	1,875
7	1,025	897	1,922
8	925	855	1,780
9	997	857	1,854
10	1,068	797	1,865
11	939	670	1,609
12	928	583	1,511
13	746	373	1,119
14	662	268	930
15	483	158	641
16	406	120	526
17	275	83	358
18	175	33	208
19	99	18	117
20	48	7	55
21	27	1	28
22	18	1	19
23 and over	24	1	25
Total	9,882	6,643	16,525
Kindergarten	1,306	1,171	2,477
Grand Total	11,188	7,814	19,002

Table 28 UAE. Male and Female Pupils. Percentages.

	1972–73	1973–74
Males per cent	61	59
Females per cent	39	41
Total	100	100

Table 29   UAE. Education for Adults.

Year	Centres number	Attendances Males	Females	Total
1972–73	54	3,446	1,466	4,912
1973–74	91	6,208	2,455	8,663

Table 30   Trucial States Development Fund Expenditure. (£ sterling)

Year	Approved	Spent
1956–57	31,000	27,000
1957–58	65,000	63,750
1958–59	85,000	64,325
1959–60	100,000	73,054
1960–61	130,000	85,000

Table 31   UAE. Federal Government Revenue and Expenditure. (million Dirhams)

	1972 (Actual)	1973 (Budget)	1974 (Budget)
Revenue			
Emirates Government			
Contributions	196·1	500·0	1,626·7
Other Revenue	4·8	10·0	65·0
Total Revenue	200·9	510·0	1,691·7
Expenditure			
Current	149·0	328·9	954·5
Development	14·7	181·1	737·2
Total expenditure	163·7	510·0	1,691·7

Table 32   Abu Dhabi Emirate. Government Revenue and Expenditure (million Dirhams)

Year	Revenue	Expenditure	Transfer to Capital Reserve	Surplus Revenue
1968	554	593	—	(39)
1969	681	820	—	(139)
1970	856	720	—	136
1971	1,651	1,104	229	319
1972	2,181	1,736	372	73
1973	4,212	3,391	215	606
1974	14,271	7,898	4,592	1,781

Note: Figures in brackets signify deficits.

Table 33   Banks in the UAE. 1975

Emirate	Branches approved
Dubai	92
Abu Dhabi	82
Sharjah	46
Ras al Khaimah	22
Fujairah	13
Um al Quaiwain	12
Ajman	11
Total	278

Table 34   Banks in the UAE. January 1975

Name of Bank	Number of Branches
1. National Bank of Abu Dhabi	16
2. National Bank of Dubai	7
3. Dubai Bank Limited	4
4. Commercial Bank of Dubai Limited	14
5. Alahli Bank Limited (C.S.C.)	1
6. Bank of Oman Limited	19
7. Bank of Sharjah	1
8. Arab Bank for Investment & Foreign Trade	1
9. Arab Bank Limited	11
10. Arab African Bank Limited	2
11. Banque Libanaise pour le Commerce S.A.	3
12. Banque du Liban et d'Outre-Mer S.A.L.	1
13. Banque du Caire S.A.E.	5
14. Rafidain Bank	1
15. Bank Saderat Iran	15
16. Bank Melli Iran	10
17. Distributors Co-operative Credit Bank	1
18. Bank of Credit & Commerce Int. S.A.	28
19. Habib Bank A.G. Zurich	9
20. Algemene Bank Nederland N.V.	4
21. Banque de Paris et des Pays Bas	2
22. Banque de l'Indochine	1
23. The British Bank of the Middle East	30
24. The Chartered Bank	10
25. Grindlays Bank Limited	10
26. First National City Bank	11
27. First National Bank of Chicago	3
28. Toronto-Dominion Bank	3
29. Habib Bank Limited	18
30. United Bank Limited	17
31. Bank of Baroda	4
32. Barclays International	3
33. Bank Omran	1
34. Janata Bank	1
35. Bank of the Arab Coast	1
36. The Royal Bank of Canada	1
37. Khalij Commercial Bank Limited	1
38. United Arab Bank	1

Table 34 (*continued*)

Name of Bank	Number of Branches
39. Investment Bank for Trade & Finance	2
40. Ajman Arab Bank	1
41. Emirates Commercial Bank	1
42. Commercial Development Bank of Sharjah	1
43. UAE Development Bank	1
44. Dubai Islamic Bank	1
Total	278

Representative Offices	
Den Norske Creditbank	1
United International Bank Limited	1
Canadian Imperial Bank of Commerce	1
Chemical Bank	1
Total	4

In January 1975 the Currency Board imposed a standstill on the opening of new banks over a period of two years, with only minor exceptions.

Table 35   Abu Dhabi. Five-year Development Plan. 1968–1972.
Annual allocations (million Dirhams)

Sector	1968	1969	1970	1971	1972
Education	42	18	21	26	15
Health	8	25	20	8	3
Agriculture	9	18	26	41	40
Industries	113	144	101	82	154
Communications	172	170	174	111	84
Municipalities	87	130	114	95	75
Housing	28	47	32	24	28
Labour	3	9	6	6	4
Information	9	12	13	16	10
Public buildings	22	37	24	8	6
Loans and investments	30	42	118	145	155
Totals	523	652	649	562	574

Table 36   Abu Dhabi. Annual Development Programmes. 1972–1974.
Budget provisions (million Dirhams)

Sectors	1972	1973	1974
Education	61	101	103
Health	18	42	93
Agriculture	19	27	32
Water, electricity & industries	217	159	299
Communications	157	145	189
Municipalities	197	245	362
Housing	24	35	85
Labour & social affairs	3	3	8
Information	13	21	30
Public buildings	41	91	151
International loans	120	76	144
Totals	870	945	1,496

Bibliography

ADAMS, MICHAEL, ed., *The Middle East: A Handbook*, Anthony Blond, London, 1971
ALBAHARNA, HUSSAIN M., *The Legal Status of the Arabian Gulf States*, Manchester University Press, 1968
BELGRAVE, CHARLES, *The Pirate Coast*, Bell, London, 1966
BIBBY, GEOFFREY, *Looking for Dilmun*, Collins, London, 1970
DANIELS, JOHN *Abu Dhabi: A Portrait*, Longman, London, 1974
FENELON, K. G., *The Trucial States—A Brief Economic Survey*, Khayats, Beirut, 2nd edition (revised), 1969
FISHER, W. B., *The Middle East*, Methuen, London, 1961
GREEN, TIMOTHY, *The World of Gold*, Michael Joseph, London, 1968
HAWLEY, DONALD, *The Trucial States*, Allen and Unwin, London, 1970
HAY, SIR RUPERT, *The Persian Gulf States*, Middle East Institute, Washington, 1969
HOURANI, GEORGE, *Arab Seafaring*, Khayats, Beirut, 1963
KELLY, J. B., *Eastern Arabian Frontiers*, Faber, London, 1964
LONGRIGG, S. H., *Oil in the Middle East*, Oxford University Press, 1961
LONGRIGG, S. H., *The Middle East: A Social Geography*, Aldine Press, Chicago, 1964
MANN, CLARENCE, *Abu Dhabi: Birth of an Oil Shaikhdom*, Khayats, Beirut, 2nd edition, 1969
MILES, S. B., *The Countries and Tribes of the Persian Gulf*, Frank Cass, London, 2nd edition, 1966
O'SHEA, RAYMOND, *The Sand Kings of Oman*, Methuen, London, 1947
OWEN, RODERIC, *The Golden Bubble*, Collins, London, 1957
THESIGER, WILFRED, *Arabian Sands*, Longman, London, 1959
WILSON, SIR ARNOLD, *The Persian Gulf*, Clarendon Press, London, 1928

Abu Dhabi Statistical Abstracts, Volume 1 (1969), Volume 2 (1973), Volume 3 (1974), Planning Department, P.O. Box 12, Abu Dhabi
Abu Dhabi News (Weekly), Ministry of Information and Tourism, P.O. Box 17, Abu Dhabi (now *Emirate News*, daily)
Dubai External Trade Statistics (Monthly), Statistics Office, Central Accounts Section, Dubai

Index

Please note that the Arabic article *Al* has been disregarded in the alphabetical order.

159

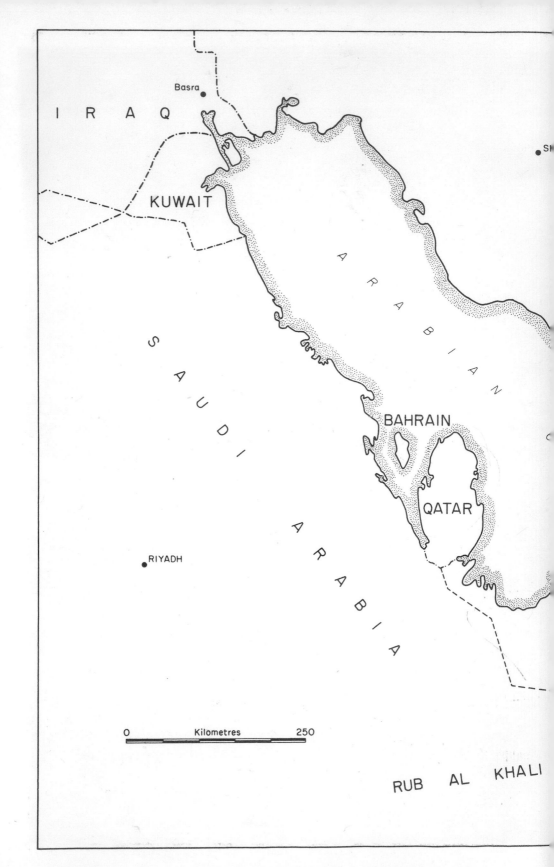

IRAQ

Basra

KUWAIT

SH

ARABIAN

SAUDI

BAHRAIN

ARABIA

QATAR

RIYADH

0   Kilometres   250

RUB   AL   KHALI